FLOUR POWER

CHRISTINE BRADY

FLOUR POWER

The Art of Cooking with Flour

ELM TREE BOOKS

LONDON

First published in Great Britain 1979
by Elm Tree Books/Hamish Hamilton Ltd
Garden House 57-59 Long Acre London WC2E 9JZ

Copyright ©1979 by Christine Brady

British Library Cataloguing in Publication Data
Brady, Christine
  Flour power.
  1. Baking   2.   Flour as food
  I.   Title
  641.6'3'11   TX763
  ISBN 0-241-10168-9

Filmset by Pioneer
Printed and bound in Great Britain by
Redwood Burn Ltd, Trowbridge and Esher

CONTENTS

INTRODUCTION

This is a book about flour and will, hopefully, tell you all you want to know but didn't know how to find out.

In this book simple terms are explained so that you know why various things happen; how to create the right environments and how to avoid those costly mistakes.

While no one wants to go back to the classroom to understand the various whys and wherefores of cooking, it does help to understand a bit of the knowledge behind all the techniques and this is what this book is all about.

My grateful thanks go to the Flour Advisory Bureau who provided background information and tested some of the recipes, and to my ex colleague, Angela Nilsen who wrote the chapter on Yeast cooking. The Butter Council and The Honey Bureau also were most helpful in testing some recipes.

Metric measurements may vary from recipe to recipe, and it is essential to follow *either* imperial or metric measures throughout any one recipe. It's perfectly possible to specify 8-oz quantities in two recipes and have one convert to 200g and the other to 225g; this is of particular importance with, for example, pastry, where exact quantities are necessary to achieve the correct flour/fat ratio.

Types of Flour

Plain Flour For short pastry, some types of cake and biscuits.
Self Raising This is a soft plain flour with baking powder added. It is used for plain cakes and scones.
Strong Plain Flour This is best for batters, yeast pastry and for puff and flaky pastry.
Wheatmeal 80-90 per cent extraction, that is with the coarser bran particles removed.
Wholemeal 100 per cent extraction, that is, with nothing removed.
Wholewheat The same as wholemeal, that is with nothing removed.
Stoneground Usually 100 per cent wholemeal.

Storing Flour

Flour has a much shorter storage life than one might expect, even under ideal conditions.

Store flour in its bag on a cool, dry airy shelf. If your kitchen is damp or steamy keep flour in a stoppered storage jar or a sealed container. Don't add new flour to old.

Plain flour keeps for 4-6 months under these conditions, self-raising flour for 2-3 months. Buy wholemeal flour in small quantities as it should only be kept for about 2 months.

Shortcrust, rich shortcrust, cheese or walnut pastry

How to achieve the best results

1 The object in making pastry is to form a light, firm but tender crust for a wide variety of sweet or savoury fillings.

2 A plain softish flour is best for pastry. This contains less gluten than the strong wheat flours and a better result will be obtained.

3 Various fats can be used: butter, margarine, lard, vegetable shortening or oil. The best for general purposes, to give both a good flavour and texture are half butter or margarine and half lard.

4 Keep all the ingredients cool. This is particularly important on a warm day. If fat gets too warm, put the bowl into the refrigerator for ten minutes or so before continuing mixing the fat into flour.

5 Rub fat into flour lightly. Just touch it and let it drop lightly, don't knead it between your fingers. If you blend it in a mixer don't let it go too long or the pastry will spoil.

6 The water when added should be as cold as possible. Sprinkle it over the top and don't pour it all in one place. If you have a glass or china rolling pin that can be filled with water, that also helps to keep the pastry cool when rolling out.

7 Don't over handle the pastry once it is mixed with water. Stir to mix but don't go on after it is all together. I've always found a wooden salad fork an excellent aid to quick mixing the pastry after rubbing in.

8 Roll out the pastry gently, in short sharp thrusts, turn pastry not rolling pin to avoid overstretching.

9 Allow the pastry to rest for about 15 minutes after it has been rolled out and you will avoid the shrinking that sometimes happens if pastry has been overstretched. It also allows the fat to harden and a better result will be achieved in the baking.

10 Lift pastry over a rolling pin or palette knife rather than with your fingers when you come to line your dish. Press gently into

1

the corner using a spare piece of pastry to push it gently into the line of the flan or pie plate.

A plain rim is customary for savoury dishes and a fluted one for sweet recipes.

11 Bake pastry in a fairly hot oven at first. In this way the water turns to steam, the starch grains burst and absorb the fat and the pastry is tender. Depending on the fillings, the temperature can be reduced after the first 15 minutes or so. For long baking, such as steak and kidney pie for example, the pastry can be covered to prevent over browning.

Know the Language

Pastry making has a secret language all its own, and if you're not in the know it can be downright bewildering.

Rubbing in: the term used for mixing fat with flour. To keep pastry light mix in the flour and fat by rubbing lightly with the fingertips and lifting the hands as you do so. This makes certain that air is mixed in and ensures a light result. By all means use an electric mixer if you have one but don't over mix.

Baking blind: this means baking a pastry case without the filling. It is sometimes partially baked, and the filling added then returned to the oven. To prevent the bottom of the case rising during cooking it is usually weighted down with a greaseproof paper or foil lining filled with butter beans. They can be used over and over again, although they cannot be cooked for themselves after they have been used in this way.

Knocking up: the term used for sealing pastry edges together such as in pies or pasties. Dampen one edge of the pastry with water, press the other edge on top, then pinch with the fingers to give a fluted effect or thicken the pastry edge by cutting it with the back of the knife.

Shortcrust Pastry

For everyday purposes shortcrust pastry is the most widely used. It shouldn't be despised on the grounds of its common use, however. It makes an excellent pie crust for a wide variety of both savoury and sweet fillings.

Simple variations of shortcrust pastry are rich shortcrust in which an egg yolk and sugar are added, and cheese pastry used either for cheese straws or for a cheese pastry to go with fish or vegetable fillings. The basic recipe for shortcrust pastry is half fat to flour.

2

200g (8 oz) plain flour
2.5ml (½ level teaspoon) salt
100g (4 oz) fat, generally half butter, half lard (see general notes)
30-45ml (2-3 tablespoons) cold water. This cannot be forecast
accurately as it depends on the absorbency of the flour

Sieve flour and salt into a bowl. Cut fat into small pieces then rub in gently, using only fingertips and keeping the mixture as cool as possible. While rubbing in, lift the hands above the bowl so that air is mixed in with the flour. This will make for a lighter result.

When the mixture resembles fine breadcrumbs, mix in the water. Sprinkle it over the flour rather than pouring it in one place only as this distributes the liquid more evenly and will avoid a streaky appearance in the pastry. Mix together until it all holds together then turn out on to a floured board and knead lightly and just sufficiently to make the pastry feel smooth. Finish it in roughly the shape you want it to be for rolling out — i.e. a round for a flan, oblong if required and so on. After rolling it to required shape allow it to 'rest' in a cool place for about 15 minutes if you can. This will ensure the pastry doesn't shrink during the cooking. Bake it at 200°C (400°F)/Gas 6 for about 15-20 minutes. If the filling requires longer cooking reduce heat and continue according to the recipe.

Rich Shortcrust
Used for sweet flans and pies and tartlets.

200g (8 oz) plain flour
2.5ml (½ level teaspoon) salt
100g (4 oz) butter or margarine
25g (1 oz) caster sugar
1 egg yolk
about 15ml (1 tablespoon) cold water

Sift flour and salt. Cut butter into small pieces and rub in with the fingertips until mixture resembles fine breadcrumbs. Add sugar and stir evenly into mixture. Blend egg yolk and water together and mix into pastry to make a firm dough. Turn out on to a floured board and knead lightly. Continue as normal shortcrust pastry.

The white of egg can often be used for glazing the pastry of a sweet pie, in which case, paint the egg white over the top and dredge with caster sugar before baking.

Cheese Pastry

Use as a flan case for fish or vegetable flans. Use the maximum quantity of cheese to make cheese straws or biscuits.

200g (8 oz) plain flour
2.5ml (½ level teaspoon) salt
1ml (¼ teaspoon) cayenne pepper
100g (4 oz) butter or margarine
1 egg yolk
about 15ml (1 tablespoon) cold water
50-100g (2-4 oz) hard, finely grated cheese — use Parmesan or
*   stale Cheddar or a mixture of both*

Make as ordinary shortcrust pastry, adding the cheese after fat and flour have been mixed.
Blend egg yolk with the water to bind the pastry.
Bake as for shortcrust pastry.

Walnut Pastry

This has an interesting texture and is well worth using for a wide variety of dishes, especially vegetarian flans. It is also pleasant with strongly flavoured fruits such as blackcurrants.

150g (6 oz) wholemeal flour
2.5ml (½ teaspoon) salt
75g (3 oz) butter
25g (1 oz) finely chopped walnuts
1 egg
water to mix

Sift flour and salt. Rub in butter until mixture resembles fine breadcrumbs. Sprinkle in finely chopped walnuts. Beat egg until yolk and white are blended then add just enough cold water to make a firm mixture. Roll out to line a 20cm (8 in) flan case and bake blind at 200°C (400°F)/Gas 6 for 15-20 minutes. Add the filling and reheat at around 160°C (325°F)/Gas 3 or according to individual recipes.

Turkey and Apricot Flan

This is an ideal recipe for using up Christmas leftovers. But it is quite easy to make on other days, and the sweet-sour taste really is very 'moorish'.

For the pastry:

    150g (6 oz) plain flour
    37.5g (1½ oz) butter
    37.5g (1½ oz) lard
    pinch salt

For the filling:

    100g (4 oz) apricots previously soaked for 3-4 hours
    45ml (3 tablespoons) sage and onion stuffing
    350g (12 oz) cooked turkey
    25g (1 oz) butter
    25g (1 oz) flour
    250ml (½ pt) chicken stock
    75g (3 oz) grated Cheddar cheese

Preheat the oven to 190°C (375°F)/Gas 5. Sift the flour and salt into a bowl, and add the fat cut into small pieces. Blend with your fingertips until the mixture resembles fine breadcrumbs, then mix with water to form a firm dough. Roll out and line 20cm (8 in) flan dish. Prick the base with a fork, fill the centre with greaseproof paper and rice or beans to hold down the pastry. Bake blind for 15 minutes. Remove from the oven and reduce heat to 160°C (325°F)/Gas 3.

Poach the apricots in a small amount of water for 10-15 minutes. Drain and roughly chop them and arrange them on the bottom of the flan case.

Make up the sage and onion stuffing and spread this over the apricots. Top with the flaked turkey and season well.

Melt the butter in a saucepan, remove from heat and stir in the flour. Add the stock gradually, stirring well to avoid lumps. Reheat, stirring continually until the sauce thickens. Pour over the mixture in the flan case. Put in the oven for 20 minutes. Just before serving, sprinkle grated cheese on top and brown under the grill. Serve at once.

Orange Flan
This flan can be served hot or cold depending on the weather.

For the pastry:

150g (6 oz) plain flour
2.5ml (½ teaspoon) salt
75g (3 oz) butter

For the filling:

3 oranges
250ml (½ pt) diluted orange squash
50g (2 oz) semolina
25g (1 oz) butter
2 standard eggs
100g (4 oz) caster sugar

To make the pastry case, sift the flour and salt into a bowl and rub in the butter with your fingertips until the mixture resembles fine breadcrumbs. Add enough water to mix to a stiff dough. Roll out to line a 17.5cm (7 in) flan dish and bake 'blind' at 190°C (375°F)/Gas 5 for about 15 minutes. Remove and allow to cool.

Peel and coarsely chop the oranges. Put the orange squash into a saucepan, scatter over the semolina and stir over a gentle heat until the liquid thickens. Leave to cool, then beat in the softened butter. Separate egg whites from yolks. Beat in egg yolks and 50g (2 oz) sugar. Add the chopped orange segments. Turn down the oven to 150°C (300°F)/Gas 2.

Whisk the egg whites until they form peaks. Fold in one-third of the remaining sugar and beat again until mixture is satiny. Then add half the remaining sugar, beat again, and sprinkle over the rest of the sugar. Pour the orange mixture into the pie case, pile meringue on top and set meringue in the fairly cool oven for about 20 minutes.

Mackerel and Spinach Flan

For the pastry:

150g (6 oz) wholemeal flour
2.5ml (½ teaspoon) salt
75g (3 oz) butter
25g (1 oz) finely chopped walnuts
1 egg
water to mix

For the filling:

1 large mackerel (or a large can of mackerel)

450g (1 lb) spinach
knob butter
little grated nutmeg
50g (2 oz) grated cheese

Preheat oven to 190°C (375°F)/Gas 5. Sift the flour and salt into bowl. Rub in the butter with your fingertips until the mixture resembles fine breadcrumbs. Add the finely chopped walnuts. Beat the egg until yolk and white are thoroughly mixed, then add to dry ingredients with sufficient cold water to make a firm mixture. Roll out to line a 20cm (8 in) flan case. Prick the bottom with a fork and cover with greaseproof paper. Fill with beans or lentils to weigh down the pastry, then bake in the oven for 15 minutes. This is known as baking 'blind'. Remove from the oven, and take out lentils and greaseproof paper. Clean and de-gut the mackerel, and poach in a little water until cooked — about 15 minutes depending on the size of the fish.

Wash the spinach thoroughly under running water. Put a knob of butter in a pan and add the spinach. Cover tightly and cook on a very low heat for about ten minutes, shaking the pan from time to time to avoid sticking. When cooked, drain and press spinach between two plates to extract as much moisture as possible. Sprinkle grated nutmeg over it, then spread in the bottom of the flan case. Flake the fish and spread over the top. (If using canned mackerel drain excess oil from can before using.) Heat in a warm oven at 160°C (325°F)/Gas 3 for 20 minutes. Heat the grill sprinkle grated cheese over the flan and brown under the grill before serving, taking care not to burn the pastry.

Spiced Rhubarb Tart
If you are using forced rhubarb this amount of sugar is just right. If your rhubarb comes straight from the garden, add extra sweetening.

For the pastry:

150g (6 oz) plain flour
75g (3 oz) butter
15ml (1 tablespoon) caster sugar

For the filling:

450g (1 lb) rhubarb
25g (1 oz) flour
50g (2 oz) caster sugar

7

2.5ml (½ teaspoon) ground cinnamon
1 125ml (¼ pt) carton natural yoghurt

Preheat oven to 200°C (400°F)/Gas 6. To make the pastry, sieve flour and rub in butter until the mixture resembles fine breadcrumbs. Add sugar, then enough water to make a firm dough. Line a 17.5cm (7 in) flan case with the pastry.

Top and tail rhubarb and cut into 2.5cm (1 in) pieces. Put in the base of the flan. Mix flour with sugar and cinnamon, stir in yoghurt and pour over the rhubarb. Bake for 30 minutes.

Apple Cheese Tart
Cheese pastry is unusual, and very good done this way with apple purée. Do sweeten to taste, as some people might find the flavour rather tart.

For the pastry:

> *150g (6 oz) cream cheese*
> *150g (6 oz) butter*
> *150g (6 oz) wholemeal flour*

For the filling:

> *450g (1 lb) cooking apples*
> *25g (1 oz) butter*
> *15ml (1 tablespoon) water*
> *rind and juice of ½ lemon*
> *12 ground cloves*
> *50g (2 oz) caster sugar*

To make the pastry, beat the cream cheese and butter together and when well blended beat in the flour. Allow the mixture to chill a little.

For the apple purée, cut and core but don't peel the apples. Put the butter and water at the bottom of the pan and then add the apples. Cover with a tight-fitting lid and cook over a low heat until the apples are really soft. Shake the pan from time to time and check to ensure they don't stick to the bottom. Sieve through a Mouli if you have one, or if not press through a sieve using the back of a wooden spoon. Add grated rind and lemon juice, the ground cloves and the sugar.

Preheat the oven to 180°C (350°F)/Gas 4. Roll out and press the pastry around the sides and bottom of a 20cm (8 in) flan dish. It is crumbly at this stage, but press together as necessary. Pour in the apple purée and cook in the oven for 40 minutes. Serve with plenty of cream.

Liver and Bacon Pie

> 275g (10 oz) shortcrust pastry
> milk to brush pastry
> 25g (1 oz) butter
> 350g (12 oz) pig's liver
> 225g (8 oz) pork sausage meat
> 100g (4 oz) streaky bacon
> 1 medium onion
> 100g (4 oz) mushrooms
> 30ml (2 tablespoons) sage and onion
> stuffing mix
> 1 egg
> seasoning

Preheat oven to 200°C (400°F)/Gas 6. Melt butter in a pan and fry liver for about eight minutes. Remove. Brown sausage meat and cook bacon for five minutes. Remove. Chop onion finely and fry until soft and golden but not brown. Chop or mince liver finely. Chop bacon, remove rind and gristle and add liver together with sausage meat, onions, chopped mushrooms, sage and onion stuffing and seasoning. Beat egg and add to rest of ingredients.

Reserving one third of pastry for lid roll out rest to line a 20cm (8 in) round pie dish. Turn filling into dish, spread evenly then cover with pastry lid. Dampen edges and seal together by pressing both edges of pastry with thumb and finger. Make leaves out of any leftover pastry, position them, then brush with milk.

Bake at 200°C (400°F)/Gas 6 for 30 minutes. Cover top of pie and continue to cook for a further 25 minutes. Serve cold with salad.

Savoury Lattice Tart

> 200g (8 oz) shortcrust pastry
> 2 medium onions
> 30ml (2 tablespoons) vegetable oil
> 200g (8 oz) minced beef
> 200g (8 oz) pork sausagemeat
> salt, pepper
> 2 cloves garlic, chopped finely
> 15ml (1 tablespoon) Soy sauce
> 30ml (2 tablespoons) flour
> 30ml (2 tablespoons) tomato purée

Preheat oven to 200°C (400°F)/Gas 6. Portion off one quarter of the shortcrust pastry for the lattice top. Roll out remaining to line a 20cm (8 in) flan case. Bake pastry case blind for ten minutes.

Chop onions finely and fry in oil until soft but not brown. Add meat and fry until meat turns colour. Add seasoning, garlic, Soy sauce and tomato purée with the flour. Stir then cover and cook very gently for 20 minutes. Cool.

Arrange meat in the flan case and roll out remaining pastry. Cut in strips and form a lattice over the top. Brush with milk and bake in a moderate oven, 190°C (375°F)/Gas 5 for about 25 minutes, or until pastry is browned.

Prawn Quiche (for 5-6)
A pleasant, light supper dish that makes a few prawns go a long way.

For the cheese pastry:

> *200g (8 oz) plain flour*
> *pinch salt*
> *1ml (¼ teaspoon) cayenne pepper*
> *100g (4 oz) margarine*
> *50g (1 oz) finely grated cheese — use a mixture of Cheddar and*
> *   Parmesan if you can. Make sure cheese is dryish*

For the filling:

> *1 litre (2 pt) fresh prawns (or 1 can peeled prawns and 250ml*
> *   (½ pt) fresh prawns mainly for garnish)*
> *3 grade 4 eggs*
> *250ml (½ pt) milk*
> *125ml (5 fl oz) carton single cream*
> *50g (2 oz) grated Cheddar cheese*
> *bunch watercress*

To make the pastry, sift flour, salt and pepper into a bowl and rub in the margarine until mixture resembles fine breadcrumbs. Stir in the cheese. Mix with cold water to make a stiff dough. Roll out to line a 25cm (10 in) flan ring. Set oven to 190°C (375°F)/Gas 5.

Peel prawns if fresh, set aside about six or seven whole ones for the garnish. Drain prawns if using canned ones. Put them at the bottom of the flan. Beat the eggs, then add the milk, cream and cheese. Pour into the flan and bake in the centre of the oven for about 35-40 minutes, until quiche is set. Wash and trim watercress and arrange it around the outside top of the flan and put the prawns around at intervals. Serve at once with tomato salad and potatoes baked in their jackets.

Variations of this recipe abound and if you add a can of asparagus spears to the flan, by placing the spears in a cartwheel in the centre, it looks very special indeed.

Tuna fish can be used instead of the prawns to make a very tasty savoury flan. Put rings of tomato and raw onion on top of the watercress to finish off the garnish.

Carrot Flan

175g (7 oz) shortcrust pastry
2 large onions
25g (1 oz) butter
200g (8 oz) carrots
100g (4 oz) finely grated Cheddar cheese
2 grade 2 eggs
250ml (½ pt) milk
salt, pepper, nutmeg

Preheat oven to 200°C (400°F)/Gas 6. Roll out pastry to line a 20cm (8 in) flan case. Bake pastry blind in top half of oven for 15 minutes. Remove and allow to cool. Chop onions finely, melt butter in a pan and fry onions gently until soft and golden but not brown. Drain fat from onions and spread evenly along the bottom of the flan case. Top and tail carrots, scrape outer skin and peel into very fine rings — use a mandolin if you have one. Sauté the carrots in the remaining butter, add more if necessary — the object is to soften them slightly and if you have cut them really thinly this will only take a short time. Spread the grated cheese over the onions in the flan case, then arrange the carrot rings in circles to cover. Beat the eggs, add milk and salt and pepper then pour into the flan case. Grate a little nutmeg over the top and put the flan case in the centre of the oven, 180°C (350°F)/Gas 4, for 15-20 minutes or until flan has set.

Turkey and Asparagus Flan

150g (6 oz) shortcrust pastry
200g (8 oz) cooked chopped turkey
298g (10½ oz) can cut asparagus
3 grade 3 eggs
250ml (½ pt) milk
50g (2 oz) finely grated cheese

Heat oven to 200°C (400°F)/Gas 6. Roll out pastry to line a 17.5cm (7 in) flan dish. Put the turkey in the bottom and season well. Drain liquid from asparagus spears and arrange them over the turkey. Mix eggs and milk together and pour over the flan. Cook for 20 minutes until pastry is golden and flan just set. Sprinkle cheese over top and put under a preheated grill just before serving.

Sardine and Green Pepper Flan

> *150g (6 oz) shortcrust pastry*
> *medium onion*
> *25g (1 oz) butter*
> *can sardines*
> *1 egg*
> *125ml (¼ pt) milk*
> *salt, pepper*
> *50g (2 oz) grated cheese*
> *½ green pepper*

Preheat oven to 200°C (400°F)/Gas 6. Roll out pastry to line a 17.5cm (7 in) flan tin. Bake blind for ten minutes. Remove from oven. Chop onion finely and fry in butter until soft and golden. Drain oil from sardines. Put onions at the bottom of the flan and mashed sardines over them. Season with pepper and a little salt. Beat egg with milk and pour over the flan. Return to oven, heat lowered to 190°C (375°F)/Gas 5 for 25 minutes or until set. Sprinkle with grated cheese and brown carefully under a grill. Cut pepper into very thin rings, removing the seeds, then arrange them over the top of the flan.

Fidget Pie

> *shortcrust pastry made from 200g (8 oz) flour*
> *450g (1 lb) potatoes*
> *2 onions*
> *450g (1 lb) cooking apples*
> *6 rashers streaky bacon*
> *seasoning*
> *250ml (½ pt) stock*

Preheat oven to 200°C (400°F)/Gas 6. Use two thirds pastry to line a 20cm (8 in) pie plate. Parboil potatoes and cut into fairly thick

12

slices. Chop onions finely. Peel core and slice cooking apples. Trim rind and gristle from bacon and chop in pieces.

Put a layer of apples at bottom of pastry then chopped onion and bacon followed by a layer of potato. Season well then repeat layer. Pour in the stock, roll out the remaining pastry to make the pie top and seal edges firmly together. Make three slits in the centre. Brush pastry with milk and bake at 200°C (400°F)/Gas 6 for 15 minutes, then turn oven down to 160°C (325°F)/Gas 3 and bake for a further 45 minutes.

Vegetarian Flan

150g (6 oz) shortcrust pastry made with wholemeal flour
medium onion
25g (1 oz) butter
3 or 4 sticks of celery
2 (grade 4) eggs
125ml (¼ pt) milk
75g (3 oz) finely grated cheese
5ml (1 teaspoon) mustard powder
salt and pepper

Preheat oven to 200°C (400°F)/Gas 6. Roll out pastry and line a 17.5cm (7 in) flan ring. Bake blind for ten minutes. Chop onion finely and fry in butter until soft and golden. Cut celery into 2.5cm (1 in) lengths and add to onion and fry for two to three minutes. Put into bottom of the flan. Beat eggs until whites and yolks are blended, add milk and grated cheese. Season with mustard, salt and pepper and pour into flan case. Bake at 190°C (375°F)/Gas 5 for about 20 minutes or until golden brown and firm to touch.

Smoked Haddock Quiche
This is a very pleasant, tasty supper dish for about 5 — 6

200g (8 oz) shortcrust pastry
450g (1 lb) smoked haddock
little milk (about 125ml/¼ pt)
3 large (grade 2 eggs)
125ml (¼ pt) single cream
parsley
seasoning

Line a 25cm (10 in) flan ring with pastry. Leave in a cool place to

13

relax. Preheat the oven to 200°C (400°F)/Gas 6. Poach the haddock in a mixture of milk and water, about half and half. When cooked retain the liquid and flake the fish carefully removing any skin and bones. Beat the eggs, add the cream and 250ml (½ pt) of the fish liquid. If you don't have 250ml, make it up with extra milk. Put the haddock at the bottom of the flan case, season well with black pepper. Pour over the liquid, sprinkle with chopped parsley and bake in the centre of the oven for 15 minutes, then reduce heat to 180°C (350°F)/Gas 4 for a further 25-30 minutes or until flan is set.

Serve with baked jacket potatoes and a green salad.

Pumpkin Flan

This is an acquired taste to my mind, as without plenty of spice it can seem very bland. However, many keen gardeners grow them so here is a recipe to make a change from roasting them with meat.

For the pastry:

75g (3 oz) plain white flour
75g (3 oz) wholemeal flour
75g (3 oz) butter
25g (1 oz) soft brown sugar
1 egg yolk
30ml (2 tablespoons) water

For the filling:

pumpkin weighing about 3 lb (1½kg)
50g (2 oz) brown sugar
5ml (1 teaspoon) cinnamon
5ml (1 teaspoon) mixed spice
1 egg

Peel pumpkin, remove pith and seeds. Cut into smallish pieces and steam in a colander over a pan of hot water for about 15 minutes. Mash the pulp then beat in the sugar and spices and beaten egg. Set on one side. Set oven at 190°C (375°F)/Gas 5. Sift both flours into a bowl and rub in the butter until mixture resembles fine breadcrumbs. Stir in sugar. Mix in egg yolk and water and bind pastry together. Roll out to fit a 17.5cm (7 in) flan case. Pour in the pumpkin mixture and use any remaining pastry pieces to make some small decoration in the middle. Bake just above the centre of the oven for about 30 minutes.

Serve with cream.

14

Bakewell Tart

A classic tart that can be served as a cake or as a dessert with cream.

For the pastry:

150g (6 oz) plain flour
75g (3 oz) butter

For the filling:

30ml (2 tablespoons) raspberry jam
50g (2 oz) butter
50g (2 oz) caster sugar
50g (2 oz) ground almonds
50g (2 oz) flour
1 large egg
15ml (1 tablespoon) or slightly more of milk

Preheat oven to 190°C (375°F)/Gas 5. Make pastry in the usual way. Roll out to line a 17.5cm (7 in) flan tin. Spread the bottom with raspberry jam. Mix all the rest of the filling together by blending butter and caster sugar until soft. Then stir in ground almonds, flour and egg. Add a little milk to make a mixture that is easy to spread. Pour into flan case, spread the top smooth, then bake in the centre of the oven for about 35 minutes.

Banana Cream Pie

The pastry case and cold custard can be prepared in advance which means this dessert can be made up very quickly.

17.5cm (7 in) cooked pastry case
250ml (½ pt) thick, cold custard
125ml (¼ pt) double cream
3 bananas

Beat the custard and the cream together until smooth and very well blended. Slice two of the bananas and lay the slices in the bottom of the pastry case. Pour over the custard cream, then put the remaining banana in slices around the edge. Serve immediately or, if not, dip the bananas used for decoration in lemon juice to prevent them turning brown.

Pineapple Cheese Tart

1 pastry case made from 150g (6 oz) rich shortcrust pastry cooked
in a 17.5cm (7 in) flan case
1 can 383g (13 oz) pineapple slices
1 pineapple jelly
200g (8 oz) natural cottage cheese
125ml (¼ pt) carton natural yoghourt

Open can of pineapple, drain the syrup into a bowl and make up to 250ml (½ pt) with water. Dissolve the jelly in the syrup by heating it over a low flame. Remove from heat and cool. Gradually beat jelly into the cottage cheese, add yoghourt and beat until smooth. Pour into the flan case and allow to set. Before serving arrange the pineapple slices over the top. Serve with cream.

This tart is very quick to assemble if you can make the flan case the day before.

Treacle Tart

shortcrust pastry made with 150g (6 oz) flour etc
150g (6 oz) golden syrup
50g (2 oz) fresh breadcrumbs grated finely
1 lemon

Preheat oven to 200°C (400°F)/Gas 6. Roll out pastry to line a 17.5cm (7 in) flan ring. Warm golden syrup, mix with breadcrumbs. Grate rind from lemon, then extract juice and add both to syrup. Pour into flan case and bake in centre of oven for 25-30 minutes.

Lemon Meringue Pie

shortcrust pastry made with 150g (6 oz) flour
25g (1 oz) cornflour
250ml (½ pt) water
25g (1 oz) margarine
50g (2 oz) caster sugar
1 lemon
2 (grade 2) egg yolks

For the meringue:

2 (grade 2) egg whites
100g (4 oz) caster sugar

Preheat oven to 200°C (400°F)/Gas 6. Line pastry to fit a 17.5cm (7 in) flan case. Bake blind for 15 minutes. Remove from oven. Mix cornflour with a little of the water to make a smooth paste, then gradually add the rest. Heat, stirring continually until mixture boils and thickens. Beat in the margarine, add sugar. Grate rind from lemon and add with the juice to the cornflour. When the mixture is cool, beat in the egg yolks. Pour into flan case. Into a grease-free bowl, put the egg whites and whisk until firm, add the sugar, one half at a time. The first can be whisked in until mixture is satiny in appearance, and the remainder should be added and just stirred in sufficiently with a metal spoon so that it is absorbed into the foam. Pile at once on to the lemon mixture and cook immediately in a cool oven, just below halfway at 150°C (300°F)/Gas 2 for about 25 minutes. The peaks of the meringue should brown slightly and the outside be crisp but the inside meringue soft. Serve cold.

Apricot Walnut Tart To serve 8 — 10

rich shortcrust pastry made with 200g (8 oz) flour etc
1, 822g (1 lb 12 oz) can halved apricots
3 eggs (grade 4 medium)
100g (4 oz) caster sugar
2.5ml (½ teaspoon) vanilla essence
50g (2 oz) walnuts
25g (1 oz) flour
30ml (2 tablespoons) sifted icing sugar

Preheat oven to 200°C (400°F)/Gas 6. Roll out pastry to line a 25cm (10 in) flan case. Bake blind at above temperature in centre of oven for ten minutes. Remove and cool. Drain apricots and reserve liquid to make a jelly or something similar. Arrange apricots rounded side uppermost in a pattern in the base of the flan. Whisk one whole egg and two yolks with the sugar until thick and creamy. Add vanilla essence, finely chopped walnuts and the sifted flour. Whisk remaining egg whites until stiff and forming peaks and fold into mixture with a metal spoon. Spoon over the apricots. Bake in a moderate oven, 180°C (350°F)/Gas 4 at below centre of oven for 20-25 minutes or until the top is firm. Allow to cool slightly then sift the icing sugar over the top.

Custard Tart

shortcrust pastry made with 150g (6 oz) flour etc
2 (grade 2) eggs
25g (1 oz) caster sugar
250ml (½ pt) milk
grated nutmeg

Preheat oven to 200°C (400°F)/Gas 6. Line a 17.5cm (7 in) flan case with the pastry and bake blind for 15 minutes. Remove and cool a little. Reduce oven heat to 180°C (350°F)/Gas 4. Beat eggs and sugar together. Heat the milk to blood heat, then pour over the eggs. Strain through a strainer then pour into the half cooked flan case. Sprinkle with nutmeg and bake in centre of oven for 20-25 minutes, or until custard is set.

Sardine Cheese Flan

This is a different sort of cheese pastry that gives a very pleasing result and is a little unusual. It is very easy as long as you chill it before rolling it out. In any case, if it crumbles a little, it is very easy to press back into shape and the finished result will be just as professional to look at.

For the cream cheese pastry:

100g (4 oz) butter
100g (4 oz) cream cheese
100g (4 oz) self raising flour

For the filling:

2 cans sardines in oil
25g (1 oz) raisins
2.5ml (½ teaspoon) made mustard
15ml (1 tablespoon) tomato ketchup
30ml (2 level tablespoons) sweet pickle

To make the pastry, cream butter until soft then beat in the cream cheese gradually until smooth. Add the flour slowly, a little at a time, until a smooth dough is formed. Wrap in foil or cling wrap and chill. Roll out to line a 17.5cm (7 in) flan case.

Preheat oven to 200°C (400°F)/Gas 6. To make the filling, drain the oil from the sardines, put them in a basin and mash with a fork. Add all the other ingredients. Pour into the flan case, smooth the top,

18

then bake just above the centre of the hot oven for about 15-20 minutes.

Cheese Straws

100g (4 oz) plain flour
2.5ml (½ level teaspoon) salt
pinch cayenne pepper
50g (2 oz) butter or margarine
50g (2 oz) very finely grated stale Cheddar or Parmesan cheese,
½ egg yolk
white of egg and chopped parsley (optional)

Preheat oven to 180°C (350°F)/Gas 4. Sieve flour salt and cayenne pepper into a bowl. Cut up the butter or margarine and rub in with the fingertips until mixture resembles fine breadcrumbs. Stir in cheese. Mix the egg yolk with a little water, about 10ml (2 teaspoons), and add to mixture to make a firm dough. Roll out the pastry to about 1cm (⅜ in) thick. Cut into even strips about 7.5cm (3 in) long and transfer carefully onto a greased baking tray. Bake in centre of oven and time carefully, about 5-7 minutes. Keep an eye on them as they burn easily. Turn out and leave to cool. For a special party, if you have the time, dip each end of the cheese straw in white of egg and then in very finely chopped parsley.

Suet crust pastry

Suet crust pastry is light and spongey and is usually steamed or boiled. It is best eaten hot and the pastry lends itself to sweet or savoury recipes. The suet can be bought shredded in packets or from the butcher when it will need some preparation. Beef suet is considered the best. Remove any membrane and grate or shred it finely, adding a little of the flour from the quantity in your chosen recipe.

For a lighter pudding breadcrumbs — fresh and finely grated — can be used in place of some of the flour.

Long, slow steaming probably gives the best results. Puddings in basins can be stood in boiling water. Well grease the basin before putting in the mixture. Cover carefully so that the water cannot reach the suet crust and allow room for it to expand by pleating the top cover of greaseproof paper. Fill the saucepan with water so that it reaches two thirds of the way up the basin and bring to the boil before adding the basin.

For roly poly puddings a steamer must be used, or failing that, you can use a colander in a saucepan with a well fitting lid. Keep the water boiling gently all the time you are steaming, and be prepared to top up with more boiling water if necessary. To cover the pudding wrap in a double layer of well greased greaseproof paper or greased foil. Seal each end by wrapping it up like a parcel.

Ginger Sponge Pudding

> *75g (3 oz) self raising flour*
> *2 teaspoons ground ginger*
> *1 teaspoon bicarbonate of soda*
> *75g (3 oz) finely grated fresh breadcrumbs*
> *75g (3 oz) shredded suet, chopped finely*

50g (2 oz) soft brown sugar
1 (grade 4) egg
75ml (about 5-6 tablespoons) milk
15ml (1 tablespoon) golden syrup

Sift flour with ginger and bicarbonate of soda into a bowl. Add breadcrumbs, suet and sugar. Beat egg and add with enough milk to make a soft dropping consistency. Well grease a 450ml(1 pt) pudding basin, put the syrup in the bottom and cover with mixture. Smooth top and cover with a pleated double sheet of greaseproof paper. Steam for two hours. Turn out and serve with warmed golden syrup.

Spotted Dick

100g (4 oz) self raising flour
100g (4 oz) finely grated fresh breadcrumbs
100g (4 oz) shredded suet
75g (3 oz) caster sugar
100g (4 oz) currants
1 (grade 4) egg
125ml (¼ pt) milk

Mix flour and breadcrumbs together and cut up suet finely and add with sugar and currants. Beat egg and add to dry mix with the milk to make a soft dropping consistency.

Well grease a 500ml (1 pt) pudding basin and fill mixture two thirds full. Smooth top and cover with a pleated double sheet of greaseproof paper or foil. Steam for about two hours.

To serve, turn out onto a warm plate and serve with thick custard.

Steak and Kidney Pudding For 6—8

This is a real old time British main meal — extremely filling, but delicious if the pastry is light and the meat is tender.

For the suet crust pastry:

200g (8 oz) self raising flour
5ml (1 teaspoon) salt
100g (4 oz) shredded suet
30ml (2 tablespoons) mixed herbs such as parsley, thyme and sage, finely chopped

For the filling:

675g (1½ lb) stewing steak
225g (½ lb) kidney
salt and pepper

Sift flour and salt into a bowl. Mix the suet with some of the flour and chop until fine then add to the rest of the flour and mix together thoroughly. Add 90ml (6-7 tablespoons) water and mix to a soft dough. Knead lightly until smooth. Turn out onto a floured board and roll out until the round will line a 2 pt greased pudding basin. Cut out a quarter wedge from the pastry and set aside to make the top.

Line the basin with the pastry and secure the cut edges of the pastry together by sealing each edge with water. Leave the pastry to rest in a cool place.

Cut up the meat into 2.5cm (1 in) chunks. If the meat is a cheap stewing cut, pre cook it for about an hour before putting it into the pudding. For the quicker cooking cuts, put it in raw. Season well. Roll out the pastry you reserved for the lid and put it on top of the meat. Seal the pastry edges together with water. Cover with greaseproof paper and make a pleat in the paper across the top to allow the pudding a chance to rise. Cover the paper with a cloth. Steam in a covered saucepan filled about two thirds up the basin with water for about two hours, depending on the meat. If it has been pre cooked two hours will be plenty, but give it longer, up to three hours if you are starting from raw meat. Don't forget to check the water level from time to time and top up with boiling water as necessary.

Meat puddings are served from the basin. Take it to the table with a napkin draped around the basin.

Dumplings

100g (4 oz) plain flour
5ml (1 teaspoon) salt
50g (2 oz) shredded suet
salt, pepper
10ml (2 teaspoons) dried mixed herbs
60ml (4-5 tablespoons) water

Sieve flour and salt into a bowl. Mix in shredded suet, seasoning and mixed dried herbs. Gradually add the water and mix to a stiff dough. Knead for a minute or two. Divide mixture into eight portions and roll each one into a small ball. Drop in to boiling liquor — usually the liquid in a meat stew and cover with a tightly fitting lid and allow to cook for about 20 minutes.

Orange Pudding
This turns the homely suet pudding into a fancy dish you can serve to guests.

> *200g (8 oz) self raising flour*
> *5ml (1 level teaspoon) salt*
> *75g (3 oz) shredded suet*
> *105ml (7-8 tablespoons) water*
> *15ml (1 rounded tablespoon) clear honey*
> *2 medium oranges*

For the sauce:

> *rind and juice of 2 oranges*
> *30ml (2 rounded tablespoons) marmalade*
> *clear honey*
> *teaspoon arrowroot*

To make the pudding sift the flour and salt into a bowl, add the finely shredded suet and mix together. Add water and mix to a soft not sticky dough. Turn out onto a floured board and knead lightly until smooth.

Take a 750ml (1½ pt) greased pudding basin and brush the inside with honey. Peel the oranges and cut into thick rounds. Press one of the rounds into the bottom and the rest to the sides of the basin, then put the suet pastry in the middle, and smooth the top. Cover with a piece of pleated greaseproof paper or foil and steam in a saucepan of boiling water for about two hours. The water should come about two thirds the way up the basin whilst boiling and will need topping up from time to time.

To serve the pudding remove from the basin carefully and invert on a serving plate.

To make the sauce, grate the rind of the two oranges and then squeeze the juice, and put in a pan with honey and marmalade. Heat slowly. Put 5ml (a teaspoon) of arrowroot in a cup and add a little of the hot liquid, stirring until smooth. Add to the rest of the liquid in the saucepan and stir over the heat until thickened. Pour into a jug and serve hot with the pudding.

Apple Crust Pudding
A very filling pudding

For the pastry:

200g (8 oz) self raising flour
(or use plain flour with 10ml (2 teaspoons) baking powder)
5ml (1 teaspoon) salt
100g (4 oz) shredded suet

For the filling:

500g (1 lb) cooking apples
45ml (3 level tablespoons) sugar

Sift flour and salt into a basin. Sprinkle in the suet and blend well together. If using fresh suet, make sure any skin has been removed and shred it mixing with the flour as you go. Add about 90ml (6-7 tablespoons) water and mix to a soft but not sticky dough. Turn out onto a floured board and knead lightly until it feels smooth.

To make the pudding, roll out pastry so that it will completely line a 1 litre (2 pt) greased pudding basin, with about 1cm overlap. Cut out a quarter wedge and reserve for the lid. Grease the basin and lift the largest piece of pastry gently into it and smooth it evenly so that it makes a smooth inner casing. Peel and core the apples into fairly thick chunks. Pack into the basin and sprinkle with sugar as you go. Now roll out the remaining pastry so that it makes a lid to cover the top completely. Dampen the edges with water and lift on top of the pudding, pinching the two pieces of pastry together so that the filling is completely enclosed.

Cover carefully with greased greaseproof paper or foil and make a pleat in the paper across the middle to allow the pastry to rise. Steam in a covered pan with water about two thirds up the basin for about 1½ hours, checking from time to time to see that the water hasn't boiled away.

To serve turn out onto a warmed plate and serve with custard or golden syrup.

Choux pastry

Steam is the main raising agent used in making choux pastry. The recipe contains a high proportion of water and this is converted into steam during baking which causes the paste to rise to three or four times its size.

A panade or thick binding sauce is the basis of the paste and eggs are beaten into it. The beating in of the eggs causes air to be added to the mixture which also makes the finished result light.

Choux pastry should be eaten the same day it is baked otherwise it becomes soggy. Although the classic use for choux pastry is for making eclairs and cream buns it makes an attractive alternative to shortcrust or flaky pastry when used with meat or fish.

> 65g (2½ oz) plain flour
> 1ml (¼ teaspoon) salt
> 25g (1 oz) butter
> 125ml (¼ pt) water
> 2 (grade 3) medium eggs

Sieve flour and salt and put on a plate or piece of paper so that it can be transferred quickly to the saucepan when the time comes. Put butter and water into a not too large saucepan. Melt butter in the water then bring the liquid to the boil. Remove from heat and add all the flour at once. Beat with a wooden spoon over a very low heat until the mixture forms a thick paste and leaves the sides of the pan. Allow to cool a little, about 4-5 minutes, then add the eggs one at a time beating them well into the mixture. At this stage the paste is smooth and definitely 'shiny' in appearance. Allow it to cool before piping.

Savoury Mince Choux
Choux pastry makes a useful extender to a cheap mince meal and

makes it look more glamorous.

2 medium onions
3 cloves garlic
30ml (2 tablespoons) vegetable oil
small piece root ginger
675g (1½ lb) minced beef
5ml (1 teaspoon) salt
5ml (1 teaspoon) mustard seed
2.5ml (½ teaspoon) EACH coriander, turmeric and chili powder
250ml (½ pt) stock
15ml (1 tablespoon) flour
50g (2 oz) raisins

For the choux pastry:

65g (2½ oz) plain flour
1ml (¼ teaspoon) salt
25g (1 oz) butter
125ml (¼ pt) water
2 (grade 3) medium eggs

Chop onion finely. Chop garlic. Heat oil in pan and add onion, garlic and ginger. Sauté until onion is transparent but not brown. Add beef and all remaining seasonings. Cook gently until meat is browned then add 15ml (1 tablespoon) flour and the stock. Bring to the boil then simmer gently for about ten minutes. Remove ginger, add raisins. Set aside.

To make the choux pastry, sieve flour and salt. Melt butter with water in a saucepan. Bring to boil then withdraw from heat and add all the flour at once. Beat rapidly with a wooden spoon over a low heat until mixture leaves the sides of the pan. Allow to cool a little, then add the eggs one at a time. Beat very rapidly to incorporate as much air as possible. The finished mixture is smooth and has a shiny satiny appearance.

Pour the minced meat into an oven proof pie dish — about 17.5cm (7 in) in diameter. Spoon the choux pastry around the edge smoothing over the top with a wet knife. Cover the centre of the mincemeat with buttered paper.

Preheat oven to 200°C (400°F)/Gas 6 then bake for 30-35 minutes until pastry is cooked right through.

26

Curried Lamb in choux pastry
This is an excellent way to use up leftover lamb.

For the choux pastry:

125ml (¼ pt) water
50g (2 oz) butter
65g (2½ oz) plain flour
2 (grade 3) medium eggs

For the curried lamb filling:

325g (12 oz) cooked lamb
15ml (1 tablespoon) curry powder
few drops Soy sauce
25g (1 oz) sultanas
little stock if necessary
15ml (1 tablespoon) chopped parsley

Preheat oven to 200°C (400°F)/Gas 6. Put the water and butter in a pan and heat to boiling. Remove from heat and pour in all the flour at once. Beat vigorously with a wooden spoon until the mixture is smooth and leaves both sides of the pan. Allow to cool a little. Beat the eggs together. When mixture has cooled add the egg, a little at a time, beating well. The mixture should be glossy and stiff when the egg has been absorbed.

Cut the lamb into small pieces and mix with curry powder, Soy sauce and sultanas. Moisten with a little stock if the meat is dry. Carefully butter a 17.5cm (7 in) pie dish, then spread the choux pastry around the edge, using the back of a spoon. Pile the lamb in the centre. Cover the lamb with buttered paper, leaving the pastry uncovered and cook for 30 minutes. Just before serving sprinkle the centre with chopped parsley.

Savoury Whiting

For the choux pastry:

125ml (¼ pt) water
50g (2 oz) butter
65g (2½ oz) plain flour
2 (grade 3) medium eggs

27

For the savoury filling:

675g (1½ lb) whiting
250ml (½ pt) milk
30ml (2 tablespoons) sage and onion stuffing
seasoning
25g (1 oz) flour
25g (1 oz) butter
50g Cheddar cheese

Preheat oven to 200°C (400°F)/Gas 6. Put water and butter in a pan and heat to boiling. Remove from the heat and pour in all the flour at once. Beat vigorously with a wooden spoon until the mixture is smooth and leaves the sides of the pan. Allow to cool a little. Beat the eggs together. When the mixture has cooled add the beaten egg a little at a time, beating hard. The mixture should be glossy and stiff when egg has been absorbed.

Poach the whiting in the milk for about 15 minutes or until the fish is just cooked. Drain, retaining the liquid. Flake the fish and sprinkle with the sage and onion stuffing and seasoning. To make the cheese sauce, melt 25g (1 oz) butter in a saucepan, remove from the heat and stir in the flour. Gradually add the liquid in which the fish was cooked, stirring so that the mixture is smooth. Heat, stirring until sauce thickens. Add cheese, then stir in fish. Butter a 17.5cm (7 in) pie dish and spread choux pastry around the edge using the back of a spoon. Pile fish in the middle. Cover fish with buttered paper leaving the pastry exposed and cook at 200°C (400°F)/Gas 6 for 30 minutes.

Profiteroles

basic choux pastry from recipe
250ml (½ pt) double cream
30ml (2 tablespoons) caster sugar

For the chocolate sauce:

50g (2 oz) plain chocolate
250ml (½ pt) water
15g (½ oz) butter
few drops vanilla essence
15ml (1 tablespoon) caster sugar

Using a 1.5cm (½ in) plain pipe, pipe the choux pastry in small puffs on to a well greased baking sheet, leaving a good space in between. Preheat oven to 200°C (400°F)/Gas 6. Bake in centre of oven for ten minutes then reduce heat to 100°C (325°F)/Gas 4 for a further 15-20 minutes. Remove from oven. Make a small slit in each bun and if the centre is not completely dry, return to the switched off oven to dry out for five minutes. Cool on a wire rack.

Whip cream, adding caster sugar and fill each bun, but not more than half an hour before serving. Pile in a shallow dish and immediately before serving pour over some of the chocolate sauce.

To make the sauce, put all the ingredients in a basin over hot water and simmer gently until blended, stirring from time to time. Pour over some of the sauce and serve the remainder separately in a dish.

Savoury choux buns
Choux pastry can also be filled with chopped chicken and ham in a Béchamel sauce. Prawns, flaked salmon or tuna also make excellent fillings.

Chocolate Eclairs
(to make about 12)

> *basic choux pastry recipe*
> *125ml (¼ pt) double cream*
> *15ml (1 tablespoon) caster sugar*
> *few drops vanilla essence*
> *chocolate glacé icing to coat*

Put the choux pastry into a piping bag with a 1,5cm (½ in) pipe fitted. Pipe fingers of the pastry about 7.5cm (3 in) long onto a greased baking sheet, leaving about 5cm (2 in) space between each.

Preheat oven to 200°C (400°F)/Gas 6. Bake eclairs at just above centre of the oven, and don't open the door for at least 20 minutes or they may collapse. Normal baking time is between 25-30 minutes depending on size.

When cooked, a tap on the base of an eclair will sound quite hollow, or if in doubt slit one down the side and see if it is cooked inside. Sometimes any damp paste inside can be scooped out with a spoon or they can be returned, slit down one side, to the oven at a lower temperature to dry out. Leave to cool on a wire rack. Make a slit down each side and fill with the cream, whipped and flavoured with sugar and vanilla essence.

29

Coat the top of each eclair with chocolate glacé icing.

For the icing, mix 25g (1 oz) cocoa with 45ml (3 tablespoons) boiling water. Sieve 200g (8 oz) icing sugar then gradually beat with the cocoa. Spoon over the top of each eclair and leave to set.

Flaky and rough puff pastry

These two pastries are basically similar but the method of achieving the end object is different. It's up to you to decide which method you prefer. The end result should be crispy flakes of pastry with air in between. It can be used for piecrusts, tarts, sausage rolls, mince pies, cream horns and so on.

Although more complicated than shortcrust, it is a delicious pastry and remarkably versatile so worth the trouble of mastering it. Lemon juice is added to the mix to work on the gluten in the flour and make it more elastic. The rolling and folding distributes the fat slightly unevenly so that when baked the pastry rises in rough flakes.

Rough Puff Pastry

> *200g (8 oz) plain flour*
> *2.5ml (½ teaspoon) salt*
> *75g (3 oz) butter*
> *75g (3 oz) lard*
> *5ml (2 teaspoons) lemon juice*
> *about 90ml (3½ fl oz) cold water*

Sieve flour and salt into a bowl. Take one quarter of the total fat and mix it into the flour until it resembles fine breadcrumbs. Cut the rest of the fat into small pieces about 6mm (¼ in) cubes then add to flour. Add lemon juice and most of the water and pour in, mixing with a palette knife until the mixture holds together. Turn onto a floured board and roll out to an oblong about 15cm x 45cm (6 x 18 in) Straighten the edges gently using a rolling pin or the palette knife. This is important if the pastry layers are to be even when finished. Mark the dough into three equal strips and fold the top over the middle and the bottom over that, straightening the edges as you go. Turn the dough so that the edges are on the right (not at the top) then roll out to the previous dimensions and repeat the folding twice more. If pastry becomes too soft when rolling, which is quite likely, allow it to chill in between. Don't flour the board too heavily to compensate as this could affect the finished quality of the pastry.

After final rolling, allow pastry to rest, then finish as for individual recipes. Bake in a hot oven at 220°C (425°F)/Gas 7 for 25 minutes. If filling requires longer cooking time, reduce oven temperature to about 170°C (325°F)/Gas 3.

Flaky Pastry

> *200g (8 oz) plain flour*
> *75g (3 oz) butter*
> *75g (3 oz) lard*
> *10ml (2 teaspoons) lemon juice*
> *about 90ml (3½ fl oz) cold water*

Sieve flour and salt into a bowl. Rub in one quarter of the total fat until mixture resembles fine breadcrumbs. Make dough, by adding lemon juice and most of the cold water to mix to a pliable dough. Turn on to a floured board and knead it lightly until it is mixed thoroughly and looks smooth. Leave it to cool in a refrigerator. Cut remaining fat into three equal portions.

Cut one third of the remaining fat into 6mm (¼ in) pieces. Roll out the dough to an oblong about 15cm by 45cm (6 x 18 in). Keep edges straight. On the top two thirds put the fat, distributing it evenly over the surface and leaving a border of about 6mm (¼ in) around the edges. Fold uncovered dough upwards and top dough over, making sure the fat adheres as you place it, and that the edges are still straight and the corners even. Turn the folded pastry to the right so that the fold is on the right. Seal the edges with a rolling pin. Repeat the rolling and distributing of fat etc twice more remembering to give the pastry a quarter turn to the right each time. For the fourth rolling, roll out to an oblong the original size, fold, turn and seal edges and allow dough to rest in a refrigerator.

Try to avoid over flouring the board during the operation. Finish according to the individual recipes. Bake at 220°C (425°F)/Gas 7 for 25 minutes, then turn down according to the filling.

Chicken and Leek Pie

> *200g (8 oz) rough puff pastry*
> *1½kg (3 lb) roasting chicken*
> *450g (1 lb) leeks*
> *salt and pepper*

30ml (2 tablespoons) parsley and thyme stuffing
egg yolk or milk to glaze

Joint the chicken. Simmer in stock or water for about 30 minutes. Set aside and leave to cool. Wash the leeks, trim and cut into 5cm (2 in) round pieces.

Remove flesh from the chicken and put it into a 17.5cm (7 in) pie dish. Add leeks, season well and sprinkle the stuffing on the top. Add 30-45ml (2 or 3 tablespoons) of the stock to moisten. Roll out the pastry to a round about 2.5cm (1 in) larger than the pie dish. Cut the outer circle off, about 1cm (½ in) deep. Press around the edge of the pie dish. Put the remaining circle of pastry on top, dampen the edges and seal to the underneath strip of pastry. Use odd trimmings to decorate and leave a slit in the middle. Brush with egg yolk or milk and cook in a preheated oven, 220°C (425°F)/Gas 7 for about 25 minutes or until pastry is golden brown.

Piggy's Puff
This is a useful recipe as it can be served hot or cold and is lovely served at a picnic.

325g (12 oz) rough puff pastry
400g (1 lb) pork sausagemeat
50g (2 oz) mushrooms
100g (4 oz) pig's liver
30ml (2 tablespoons) sage and onion stuffing
salt and pepper
10ml (2 teaspoons) Soy sauce

Preheat oven to 220°C (425°F)/Gas 7. Put the sausagemeat into a bowl. Chop mushrooms and liver finely and add to rest of ingredients. Form into a roll.

Roll out the pastry into a rectangle to fit round the meat, allowing the pastry to overlap by about 2cm (¾ in). Roll it around the meat, seal the pastry edges together firmly by dampening the edges with water and pinching together firmly to make a fluted edge on the top side. Brush with milk.

Put on a baking sheet and bake in the top half of the oven for 20 minutes. Reduce heat to 200°C (400°F)/Gas 6 and continue cooking for a further 15 minutes.

Serve cut in thick slices accompanied by green salad.

Rabbit and Lemon Pie

> 200g (8 oz) flaky pastry
> 4 rashers streaky bacon
> 1 rabbit cut into joints
> savoury mustard
> grated rind from 1 large lemon
> 250ml (½ pt) stock
> salt and pepper
> 50g (2 oz) mushrooms
> egg yolk or milk to glaze

Cut rind and gristle from bacon. Place rabbit joints in a casserole. Spread each rasher of bacon with mustard and lay them over the rabbit. Add grated lemon rind, stock and seasoning. Cook at 180°C (350°F)/Gas 4 for 1½ hours. Leave to cool, add sliced mushrooms. Preheat oven to 200°C (400°F)/Gas 6.

Transfer rabbit and most of the liquid to a deep pie dish. Roll out pastry to 2.5cm (1 in) larger than the dish. Cut away the extra 2.5cm (1 in). Dampen the rim of the dish and place the line of pastry around the edge. Dampen this then place the rest of the pastry on top. Press together firmly with the fingers. Make pastry leaves with any excess pastry. Put a slit in the middle of the pie. Brush with egg yolk or milk and bake for about 20 minutes until pastry is golden brown.

Eccles Cakes

> 200g (8 oz) rough puff pastry
> 50g (2 oz) butter
> 50g (2 oz) soft brown sugar
> 150g (6 oz) currants
> 50g (2 oz) mixed peel
> 2.5ml (½ teaspoon) grated nutmeg
> white of one egg for glazing plus a little caster sugar

Make the rough puff pastry as described. To make the filling, melt the butter and stir in remaining ingredients (except those for glazing). Set filling to one side.

Preheat oven to 220°C (425°F)/Gas 7. Roll out pastry thinly and cut into 10cm (4 in) rounds. Put 5ml (a rounded teaspoon) of the filling in the middle of each round. Dampen pastry all round the edges and draw them together, pinching them well to seal the edge. Turn over, and gently flatten with a rolling pin. Score three diagonal lines across the top of each. Put on a dampened baking sheet and brush top of cakes with egg white, sprinkle with caster sugar.

Bake for 15-20 minutes. Cool on a wire rack.

Cream Horns

>*flaky pastry made with 200g (8 oz) flour*
>*about 45ml (3 tablespoons) raspberry jam*
>*250ml (½ pt) double cream*
>*50g (2 oz) caster sugar*
>*2-3 drops vanilla essence*
>*milk and caster sugar for glaze*

Roll out pastry evenly into an oblong 20 x 25cm (8 x 10 in). Cut into eight strips 2.5cm by 25cm (1 x 10 in). Brush underside of strip with milk. Starting at the pointed end, wind each strip around the horn case so that each coil slightly overlaps the other. Press edges together as you go. Brush outside with milk and sprinkle with caster sugar. Put the final end of the horn on the underside and place on a dampened baking sheet. Leave to rest.

Preheat oven to 220°C (425°F)/Gas 7. Bake for 15-20 minutes. Gently loosen the pastry from the horn tin and cool on a wire rack.

Whip cream with caster sugar and few drops vanilla essence. When cold and just before serving, put a little raspberry jam in the bottom of the horn case and fill up with cream. If you wish you can pipe the cream in using a 1.5cm (½ in) plain tube. Dredge with more caster sugar just before serving.

Orange Horns

Vary the filling. Flavour the sweetened cream with grated orange rind and 5ml (1 teaspoon) of Grand Marnier. Omit the vanilla essence and raspberry jam.

Mixed Fruit Tart

>*flaky pastry made with 200g (8 oz) flour*
>*egg yolk for glaze*
>*mixture of fruit to provide attractive contrast in colouring, such as*
>   *strawberries or raspberries and apricots or canned peaches,*
>   *ripe gooseberries, red or black cherries, sliced bananas, black or*
>   *green grapes*
>*apricot jam for glaze*

Preheat oven to 220°C (425°F)/Gas 7. Roll out pastry to make a rectangle 15 by 25cm (6 x 10 in). Cut off the outer edge about 2cm (¾ in) wide and set aside very carefully. Lay the remaining rectangle on a dampened baking sheet. Trim the outer edge previously cut off so that it will fit on top. Mitre the edges and press gently on top of the rectangle so that it makes a narrow ledge. Prick the inside rectangle carefully and brush the top and outside edge with egg yolk.

Bake for about 20 minutes. Cool a little then brush the centre only with warmed apricot jam. Arrange the fruits in stripes across, contrasting the colours attractively. Pack fruit fairly tightly. Finally brush fruit generously with more warmed apricot jam, adding a little water to make the glaze of an easy to brush consistency.

Jam Turnovers

> *flaky pastry made with 200g (8 oz) flaky pastry*
> *75ml (5 tablespoons) whole fruit jam*
> *egg white and caster sugar to glaze*

Preheat oven to 220°C (425°F)/Gas 7. Roll out pastry to a rectangle 30 by 20cm (12 x 8 in) and then cut into 10cm (4 in) squares.

Put a spoonful of jam in the middle of each square. Dampen all round the edges with water, fold over to make a triangle, pressing the edges together firmly so that no jam escapes. Brush with egg white and sprinkle over the caster sugar.

Transfer to a dampened baking sheet and cook at top of oven for about 20 minutes. Leave to cool on a wire rack.

Puff pastry

The object in making puff pastry is to incorporate even layers of dough, air and fat together, so that when the pastry is baked the flour will absorb the fat, the air will expand and cause the pastry to rise evenly.

Because of the high proportion of fat to flour it is more difficult to handle than other pastries.

The most common use for puff pastry is in *vol au vents*, and in *milles feuilles*, it can also be used for sweet and savoury patties, *palmiers* and so on.

> *200g (8 oz) plain flour*
> *200g (8 oz) butter*
> *few drops of lemon juice*
> *5ml (1 teaspoon) salt*

Sift flour and salt into a bowl, rub in a small nut of the butter, add lemon juice and enough cold water to make a stiff dough. Transfer to a floured board and knead it well with the hands until smooth and elastic. Roll out until more than twice the size of the remaining fat. Put the fat to the top half of the pastry leaving a small overlap all round, then fold over the other half of the pastry and seal the edges. Turn the dough with the fold to the left and roll out the pastry again to make a similar rectangle as before. Fold in three, seal edge with the rolling pin, then turn to the left again and repeat. Leave to cool a little each time and repeat five times more. After the final rolling, let the pastry relax for at least 30 minutes.

Be sure to keep the sides straight and the corners square or the pastry will rise unevenly. Cut the edges with a sharp knife dipped in hot water and don't drag it as you cut.

Preheat oven to 230°C (450°F)/Gas 8. Make sure oven is thoroughly preheated and bake the pastry half way up. Small vol au vents will take about 15 minutes to cook, but larger pastry cases up to 30 minutes.

Curried Mince Triangles
To make about 8

> *1 medium onion*
> *15ml (1 tablespoon) vegetable oil*
> *1 small cooking apple*
> *225g (8 oz) minced beef*
> *15ml (1 tablespoon) fruit chutney*
> *15ml (1 tablespoon) curry powder*
> *seasoning*
> *25g (1 oz) sultanas*
> *400g (14 oz) puff pastry*

Chop onion finely. Heat oil and fry onions until soft and golden. Peel core and chop cooking apple and add to onion with minced beef. Fry until meat has just turned colour, then add chutney, curry powder and seasoning. Cook very gently, add 15ml (a tablespoon) of water if mixture looks like sticking. Cover and simmer for 10-15 minutes. Add sultanas and stir, then leave to cool.

Preheat oven to 220°C (425°F)/Gas 7. Roll out pastry thinly, and cut into eight 15cm (6 in) squares. Put some of the minced meat in the centre of each square and draw over the pastry diagonally. Seal well by dampening the edges with water and pinching together. Brush with milk and bake at top of oven for 15 minutes.

Cool on a wire rack.

Fish in Hiding

> *30ml (2 tablespoons) vegetable oil*
> *1 large onion*
> *100g (4 oz) mushrooms*
> *450g (1 lb) flaked coley with bones removed*
> *1 small, 227g (8 oz) can tomatoes*
> *5ml (1 teaspoon) mustard powder*
> *15ml (1 tablespoon) Worcestershire sauce*
> *15ml (1 tablespoon) lemon juice*
> *salt and pepper*
> *375g (12 oz) puff pastry*

Preheat oven to 200°C (400°F)/Gas 6. Heat cooking oil, chop

38

onion finely and sauté until soft and golden. Add sliced mushrooms and fry for a few minutes longer. Mix with the fish. Drain tomatoes and reserve liquid to add to soup or stock. Mash tomatoes with a fork and add to fish with the mustard, Worcestershire sauce, lemon juice and plenty of seasoning.

Roll out the pastry to a rectangle about 30 by 25cm (12 x 10 in). Pile filling in the centre and bring pastry ends up over the top. Dampen the edges and seal together by pinching with the fingers. Seal well at both ends in the same way.

Brush with milk. Bake for 15-20 minutes until pastry is golden brown. Serve with green salad in a tangy French dressing.

Jumbo Sausage Roll

> *350g (12 oz) puff pastry*
> *1 (grade 2) egg for glazing*

For the filling:

> *1 medium onion*
> *25g (1 oz) butter*
> *350g (12 oz) sausagemeat*
> *100g (4 oz) fresh white breadcrumbs*
> *1 cooking apple, peeled, cored and chopped*
> *50g (2 oz) sultanas*
> *15ml (1 tablespoon) curry powder*
> *salt and pepper*

Preheat oven to 200°C (400°F)/Gas 6. To make the filling, chop onion finely and fry in butter until soft but not browned. Stir in remaining ingredients.

Roll out puff pastry to about 25 by 30cm (10 x 12 in). Put filling in the centre, brush edges with beaten egg, then roll pastry over like a Swiss roll. Seal edges by dampening and pressing together with the fingers. Turn over so that join is underneath and place on a dampened baking sheet. Brush with egg and bake for about one hour. If pastry appears to be browning too fast, cover the top and lower heat to 180°C (350°F)/Gas 4 to allow filling to cook through.

Lamb en Croute

> *½ leg of lamb, boned*
> *3 lamb's kidneys*
> *2, 1cm (½ in) slices bread*

39

25g (1 oz) butter
30ml (2 tablespoons) chopped herbs — rosemary, parsley, thyme,
  sage
salt and pepper
350g (12 oz) puff pastry

Ask the butcher to bone the lamb for you. Remove membrane from kidneys, wash thoroughly and chop into small pieces. Grate bread, removing crusts. Melt butter in saucepan and fry kidneys gently. Add bread, chopped herbs and seasoning. Press into the cavity of the lamb.

Roll out the puff pastry thinly to make a sufficiently large square to cover the meat completely. Put the leg of lamb, pressed roughly into shape in the middle. Draw the pastry over the meat and dampen the edges then press well together so that it is completely sealed. Turn the meat over so that the join is underneath before transferring it to a dampened baking sheet.

Preheat oven to 200°C (400°F)/Gas 6. Cook for 30 minutes then lower heat to 180°C (350°F)/Gas 4 for a further 25-30 minutes.

Palmiers

200g (8 oz) puff pastry
egg white and caster sugar to glaze

Preheat oven to 230°C (450°F)/Gas 8. Roll the pastry to a rectangle 25 by 30cm (10 x 12 in). Sprinkle with caster sugar. Taking the two long ends, roll the pastry so that the two coils meet in the middle. Press lightly together. Cut into ten equal slices. Lay each slice flat and press gently with a knife so that it looks heart shaped. Brush with egg white and sprinkle with more caster sugar. Transfer to a dampened baking sheet and bake for about ten minutes, then turn them over and cook for a further five minutes.

Raspberry Cream Slices
Get all the ingredients ready, the pastry cooked, raspberries prepared, cream whipped, then assemble at the last minute. The glacé icing should be put on the top slices beforehand, but by assembling at the last minute it prevents everything looking 'soggy'.

450g (1 lb) puff pastry
45ml (3 tablespoons) raspberry jam
225g (8 oz) raspberries

40

60ml (4 tablespoons) whipped double cream
glacé icing made with 150g (6 oz) icing sugar with 30ml (2 tablespoons) lemon juice

Divide pastry in two, cutting so that you have two shapes as near square as possible. Preheat oven to 220°C (425°F)/Gas 7. Roll out each square to about 30cm (12 in) square. Prick pastry with a fork and put on a dampened baking sheet and allow to rest for 15 minutes.

Bake near top of oven for twelve minutes so that pastry is golden. Leave to cool on a wire rack.

To assemble, cut each pastry square into three 10cm (4 in) lengths using a serrated edge knife, then each strip into 6cm (2¼ in) pieces. Put twelve aside to make the top slices which will be covered with glacé icing.

To make the icing, sieve the icing sugar into a bowl, then gradually beat in the lemon juice. You may need to add a very little water as well, but don't make the icing too thin — it needs to be quite thick. Coat each top slice with the icing, using a knife dipped in hot water. Allow to set.

Just before serving mix jam with raspberries. Pile a little onto each remaining slice, spread with a knife then add a little whipped cream. Top with a pastry slice coated with icing and serve at once.

Hot watercrust pastry

This is the only pastry where the ingredients should be handled warm. This is so that the dough is pliable when being worked. All utensils should be warmed before use and the flour and salt sieved into a warm bowl.

Apart from that, be prepared to work quickly so that the pastry is moulded into the tin or around a jam jar while the warmth is still there. Egg yolk can be added to the mixture, this makes the pastry more liable to crack but makes it taste better and last longer.

> *400g (1 lb) plain flour*
> *10ml (2 teaspoons) salt*
> *150g (6 oz) lard*
> *150ml (10 tablespoons) milk and water mixed equally*
> *egg yolk (optional)*
> *egg yolk, salt and water for glaze*

Sieve flour and salt into a warm mixing bowl. Put lard and liquid into a saucepan and heat gently until fat has melted, then turn up the heat and bring to the boil. Allow to boil until mixture makes a splattering noise. Remove at once. Make a well in the centre of the flour and pour in the liquid. If using egg yolk add at this stage. With a wooden spoon draw in the flour. The heat of the liquid will partially cook the starch grains. Mix to a rough dough then use your hands as soon as the mixture is cool enough to knead until smooth, transferring it to a floured wooden board to do so. The dough, when sufficiently kneaded, should be smooth in appearance and free from cracks. It will feel more greasy than other pastry.

To mould

There are various decorative moulds that can be bought and these help you to obtain a very professional appearance with pies. They usually have a pinning device so that the tin can be taken apart making the pie easier to remove for glazing during cooking. Alternatively, use a loose bottomed cake tin. You can also mould individual pies over a jam jar as described below.

In all cases the tins or jars should be greased and floured well first.

Roll out the pastry to about 6mm (¼ in) thick. It is important to get the pastry an even thickness throughout, and to see that it isn't extra thick around the base where the bottom and sides meet. If you are using a tin, fold the pastry into a wedge shape to make it easier to handle in the tin. Reserve about a quarter of the pastry for the lid and keep it in a warm place so that it is still pliable when you are ready to use it.

Put the pastry carefully in the tin and use your hands to mould it lightly into shape. Use your knuckles rather than fingertips to press in at the base, then raising it gently up the sides as you go.

Pack with the filling, press into the edges.

Roll out the pastry for the lid. Dampen both edges of the pastry and press well together. Use any pastry trimmings to make leaves for decoration, or make small strips of the pastry into 'roses'. Leave a hole in the centre of the pie to allow the steam to escape during cooking. A pastry rose can be put in it to cover after cooking.

To Mould Over a Jar

Use a straight sided jar and make sure it is really well greased. Sprinkle it with a little flour. Reserve about a quarter of the pastry for the lid (keep warm).

Upturn the jar, roll out pastry to about 6mm (¼ in) thick. Put the pastry in the centre of the base of the jar, then using your hands mould it gently and evenly around the jar to make a pie shape. Aim to get the pastry even throughout and work up all sides evenly and gradually. Trim neatly around the top edge and leave on the jar until quite cold.

Ease the pastry off the jar gently using a round bladed knife. Pack with the filling immediately, pressing it tightly into the corners. Roll out remaining pastry for the lid. Dampen both pastry edges and press together firmly. Make a hole in the centre of the lid and decorate the top of the pie with any trimmings.

To Bake

Preheat oven to 220°C (425°F)/Gas 7. Pin a double sheet of greased greaseproof paper around each pie so that it extends about 5cm (2 in) above the top. Bake in centre of oven for about 20 minutes then reduce heat and follow individual recipes according to the fillings in each pie. After about an hour remove paper collars and brush with a glaze of egg yolk, salt and a little water and return to oven to finish cooking.

Picnic Pie

> *200g (8 oz) hot watercrust pastry*
> *200g (8 oz) minced beef*
> *200g (8 oz) pork sausagemeat*
> *30ml (2 tablespoons) chopped mixed herbs*
> *salt and pepper*
> *egg yolk, salt and water for glaze*

Preheat oven to 220°C (425°F)/Gas 7. Using a 450g (1 lb) spring tin, mould the pastry as described. Mix together the beef, sausage-meat, herbs and seasoning and pack into the pie case. Cover with a lid and decorate, leaving a hole in the centre of the pie top.

Cook for 20 minutes, then reduce heat to 180°C (350°F)/Gas 4 for a further 50 minutes. About 15 minutes from the end, remove pie from the tin carefully, glaze with egg yolk, salt and water wash and return to the oven to finish baking.

Veal and Gammon Pie

> *200g (8 oz) hot watercrust pastry*
> *325g (12 oz) lean veal*
> *1 gammon rasher weighing about 150g (6 oz)*
> *5ml (1 teaspoon) dried sage*
> *salt and pepper*
> *egg yolk, salt and water for glaze*
> *125ml (¼ pt) jellied stock*

Preheat oven to 220°C (425°F)/Gas 7. Using a 450g (1 lb) spring tin, mould the hot watercrust pastry as described, reserving a quarter of the pastry for the lid. Chop veal and gammon into small dice. Mix together with the seasonings and add a very little stock to moisten (reserve most of the stock for 'topping up' at the end).

Cover with the pastry lid, leaving a hole in the top of the lid. Cook for 20 minutes then reduce heat to 180°C (350°F)/Gas 4 and cook for a further 2-2½ hours. After about one hour at the lower temperature, remove the loaf tin, brush with egg glaze and return to oven to finish cooking.

44

Remove pie from oven, allow to nearly cool, then using a funnel, pour in the warmed jellied stock very carefully into the pie. When cold the stock will fill any vacant corner with the jelly. Leave to set really thoroughly then serve cold.

Pork Pie
Make as Veal and Gammon Pie but use 325g (12 oz) lean pork and 150g (6 oz) sausagemeat instead of the veal and gammon.

Noodle pastry

Home made noodles are easy and good fun to make. The whole family can join in helping to stretch it out all over the kitchen table.

200g (8 oz) strong plain flour
1 level teaspoon salt
2 (grade 2) eggs
15ml (1 tablespoon) olive oil
60ml (4 tablespoons) hot water

Sieve flour and salt into a bowl. Make a well in the centre, then drop in the eggs, olive oil and hot water. Stir with a wooden spoon and fork until worked together, then transfer to a floured board and knead until it is smooth and elastic to the touch. This should take about 10-15 minutes, but it must be done and is the longest part of the operation.

Wrap in a polythene bag and leave to rest for at least 15 minutes. Before rolling out, take a highly patterned teacloth or small tablecloth and lay it out over the table. Flour it lightly. Roll out the pastry over the cloth until it is thin. Leave the rolling pin to one side, then gently pull the pastry with the fingers until it is so transparent you can see the patterns in the cloth underneath. The pastry is very elastic so this isn't difficult if done with care. When it is as thin as you can make it, roll it up loosely and cut it into 6mm (¼ in) pieces. Unravel each strip carefully and hang it over the back of a chair to air for half an hour.

The quantities given are probably enough for four people depending on individual appetites. It is ample for a starter but as a main meal you may wish to increase quantities.

Home made noodles cook more quickly than shop bought ones. Boil in fast boiling salted water for about seven minutes. Stir in a generous knob of butter after draining well, and serve at once, either accompanied by grated Parmesan cheese or as an accompaniment to meat.

Ravioli

Make the noodle pastry described before. Roll out and pull gently as explained to form a large square. Brush half the square with water. Over the part you have brushed with water place teaspoonful of the filling, leaving about 3cm (1¼ in) between each one. Fold over the remaining pastry and press firmly around each mound of filling. Cut out each individual mould with a sharp knife, or better still, a fluted pastry cutter. Leave to dry out for some hours, or even overnight.

To cook, boil in plenty of boiling, salted water for at least 20 minutes. Test to see whether they are cooked and continue for another few minutes if necessary. Serve with a Tomato or Bolognese Sauce.

Fillings

Meat Filling 1

> *100g (4 oz) minced beef*
> *25g (1 oz) fresh finely grated breadcrumbs*
> *salt and pepper*
> *good pinch dried sage*

Mix all ingredients together.

Meat Filling 2

> *100g (4 oz) pork sausagemeat*
> *50g (2 oz) finely chopped ham*
> *salt and pepper*
> *good pinch chopped thyme*

Mix all ingredients together.

Vegetable Filling

> *100g (4 oz) spinach*
> *50g (2 oz) curd cheese*
> *25g (1 oz) grated Parmesan cheese*
> *salt and pepper*

If using frozen spinach, chop finely and mix with remaining ingredients to form a stiffish paste. Season well. If using fresh spinach, cook lightly and press dry between two plates, chop finely and mix with other ingredients.

47

Cannelloni

Prepare the noodle pastry as before, roll and pull out very thinly. Cut into rectangles 10 x 8cm (4 x 3 in) and use one of the fillings as described for ravioli.

Cook in boiling salted water for about 5 minutes, drain. Place some of the filling along the centre then roll and place in a fireproof dish. Cover with a Tomato or Bolognese sauce and cook for about 25-30 minutes in a moderate oven, 180°C (350°F)/Gas 4.

Apple Strudel
(enough for 6 — 8)

> *225g (8 oz) noodle pastry*
> *675g (1½ lb) cooking apples*
> *50g (2 oz) chopped almonds*
> *50g (2 oz) raisins*
> *5ml (1 teaspoon) powdered cinnamon*
> *75g (3 oz) demerara sugar*
> *50g (2 oz) butter*
> *50g (2 oz) fresh breadcrumbs*
> *icing sugar to dredge*

Preheat oven to 200°C (400°F)/Gas 6. Roll out pastry until transparently thin, as described in basic noodle pastry recipe. Leave to rest on a floured cloth.

Peel, core and thinly slice apples. Mix with almonds, raisins, cinnamon and demerara sugar.

Melt half the butter in a saucepan and stir in the fresh breadcrumbs until coated, then add them to apple mixture.

Melt remaining butter and brush the outside edges of the pastry to a depth of about 2.5cm (1 in). Put all the filling in the centre. With the help of the cloth, flick both ends of pastry over the top and seal the edges together. Transfer very carefully onto a well greased baking sheet so that the edges of the pastry are underneath. Curve it into a crescent shape. Brush with remaining melted butter and bake at the top of the oven for about 30 minutes or pastry is pale gold in colour. Dredge with icing sugar. Serve hot or cold.

Although Apple Strudel is the best known in this country, these other fillings are delicious.

BLACK CHERRY FILLING Use one 450g (1 lb) jar black cherries or equivalent in cans, draining the juice, 50g (2 oz) ground almonds, 150g (6 oz) finely grated breadcrumbs, 75g (3 oz) granulated sugar.

Mix all the ingredients together — keep the mixture fairly dry, then roll up pastry and proceed as for Apple Strudel.

CREAM CHEESE FILLING Mix 450g (1 lb) cream cheese with 2 egg yolks, 50g (2 oz) ground almonds, grated rind and juice of 1 medium lemon, 100g (4 oz) raisins. Mix well together, then roll up and proceed as for Apple Strudel.

Chappaties
An unleavened bread from India

> *225g (8 oz) wholewheat flour*
> *5ml (1 teaspoon) salt*
> *125ml (¼ pt) plus 30ml (2 tablespoons) warm water*
> *30ml (2 tablespoons) vegetable oil*

Sift flour and salt into a bowl and mix in the warm water gradually to make a soft but not sticky dough. Put onto a floured board and knead for five minutes using a rocking motion. Allow to stand for 15 minutes. Divide into eight portions and roll out each one into a thin round.

Heat the oil in a thick based frying pan and when hot, fry the chappaties one at a time, turning each over once only. They are cooked when they begin to turn colour. Drain off excess oil on kitchen paper and keep hot. Serve with curry.

Scones

Scone mix is more versatile than many people imagine. It can be used in place of a yeast dough in pizza type recipes, and a scone topping makes a quick and tasty extender to meat stews. Tea time isn't quite the same without scones dripping with butter, jam and cream.

Self raising flour is often used for scones, but plain flour with a higher than usual baking powder content can be used instead.

As a basic guideline use 200g (8 oz) flour to 20ml (4 level teaspoons) baking powder. If using self raising flour use 10ml (2 level teaspoons) baking powder instead.

Butter, or margarine as a cheaper alternative, is the best fat to give a good flavour. The proportion of fat to flour is fairly low: 75g (3 oz) fat to each 400g (1 lb) flour is usual.

Cold milk is usually used for mixing, although sour milk is excellent and gives a better rise.

Once the liquid is mixed into the flour, work speedily. When the recipe says knead, it means with the fingertips and not with the knuckles like a yeast dough.

Cook in a hot oven, though if using for a mock pizza or a cobbler type topping less heat may be necessary so as not to scorch the other ingredients.

200g (8 oz) plain flour
20ml (4 level teaspoons) baking powder
2.5ml (½ teaspoon) salt
40g (1½ oz) butter
approx 125ml (¼ pt) milk
extra milk for brushing tops of scones

Preheat oven to 230°C (450°F)/Gas 8. Sift flour with baking powder and salt into a bowl. Rub in the butter using a light fingertip until the mixture resembles fine breadcrumbs. Pour in all the milk and mix with a wooden fork or round bladed knife until mixture holds together.

Turn out on to a floured board and knead lightly with the fingertips until smooth. Roll out gently, (or use the palm of your hand) to about 2cm (¾ in) thick and cut into rounds using a pastry cutter. Put on a greased baking tray, brush tops with milk. Place near the top of the preheated oven and bake for about ten minutes.

Scones are best eaten on the same day as they are cooked.

Fruit Scones
To basic mixture add 25g (1 oz) caster sugar after mixing flour and fat. Stir in 25g (1 oz) mixed dried fruit.

Cheese Scones
Mix 2.5ml (½ teaspoon) cayenne pepper into flour, salt and baking powder, then after rubbing in fat add 50-75g (2-3 oz) finely grated cheese.

Syrup Scones
Add 5ml (1 teaspoon) mixed spice with flour. Add 15ml (1 tablespoon) golden syrup and use slightly less than 125ml (¼ pt) milk.

Mix syrup and milk by warming them slightly before mixing into flour.

Wholemeal Scones
Use half wholemeal flour with white flour. You will probably need a little extra milk in the mixing. A variety of chopped fresh herbs can be used for added flavour — parsley is particularly good. Add 15ml (1 tablespoon) finely chopped parsley after mixing fat with flour.

Scone Pizza
Make basic scone dough as described in basic recipe. Grease a baking sheet and roll out dough to make a round.

For the topping:

> *3 rashers streaky bacon*
> *6 slices salami*
> *small, 227g (8 oz) can tomatoes*
> *6 anchovy fillets*
> *10ml (2 teaspoons) oregano (optional)*

Preheat oven to 200°C (400°F)/Gas 6. Cut rind and gristle from bacon rashers and cut in two. Arrange in a wheel shape over scone mix. Into each wedge shape put a piece of salami.

Drain liquid from tomatoes and mash tomatoes before pouring over the meat. Arrange anchovy fillets on top. Sprinkle with 10ml (2 teaspoons) oregano. Bake near the top of oven for about 25-30 minutes.

Savoury Beef with Scone Topping (for 6)

> *900g (2 lb) braising steak*
> *45ml (3 tablespoons) flour*
> *2.5ml (½ teaspoon) mixed dried herbs*
> *salt and pepper*
> *10ml (1 dessertspoon) mustard powder*
> *45ml (3 tablespoons) vegetable oil*
> *375ml (¾ pt) dry cider*

For the scone topping:

> *200g (8 oz) plain flour*
> *20ml (4 level teaspoons) baking powder*
> *5ml (1 teaspoon) salt*
> *40g (1½ oz) butter*
> *10ml (2 teaspoons) dried mixed herbs*
> *approx 125ml (¼ pt) milk*

Cut meat into cubes. Mix flour with herbs, salt pepper and mustard powder and roll meat in it. Heat oil in pan and fry meat on both sides. Transfer to a casserole, add cider and cook at 180°C (350°F)/Gas 4 for about two hours or until tender. Meanwhile make the scone topping. Sift flour baking powder and salt together. Rub in butter until mixture resembles fine breadcrumbs. Sprinkle in the mixed herbs. Stir in the milk and mix to make a soft but not sticky dough. If the mixture is too dry, add a little more milk. Turn on to a floured board and cut the scone mix into rounds with a 5cm (2 in) pastry cutter.

Remove casserole from oven and turn up the heat to 200°C (400°F)/Gas 6. Put the scone rings over the top of the casserole and return without the lid to oven after you have given it about ten minutes to reach a higher temperature. Allow scone topping to cook for about 15 minutes.

Traditional Soda Bread

> 450g (1 lb) plain flour
> 5ml (1 level teaspoon) salt
> 5ml (1 level teaspoon) cream of tartar
> 5ml (1 level teaspoon) bicarbonate of soda
> 25g (1 oz) lard
> 250ml (½ pt) buttermilk or milk

Set oven at 200°C (400°F)/Gas 6. Sift flour, salt, cream of tartar and bicarbonate of soda into a bowl. Rub in lard until mixture resembles fine breadcrumbs. Make a well in the centre and gradually add the buttermilk or milk to make a soft dough. Knead lightly on a well floured board until mixture holds it shape. Form into a round. Score the top lightly three times and bake for about 35 minutes or until well risen and brown.

The joy of soda bread is that you can make it without yeast if you run out of bread over a holiday weekend or any other time. Personally I make it frequently, the wholemeal bran loaf is particularly good served at breakfast with a plain boiled egg, or for a quick lunch with cheese and a tangy pickle.

Wholemeal Soda Bread

> 350g (14 oz) wheatmeal flour
> 5ml (1 level teaspoon) salt
> 5ml (1 level teaspoon) cream of tartar
> 10ml (2 level teaspoons) bicarbonate of soda
> 50g (2 oz) bran
> 25g (1 oz) lard
> 375ml (¾ pt) buttermilk or sour milk
> 15ml (1 tablespoon) honey

Set oven at 200°C (400°F)/Gas 6. Sift flour, salt, cream of tartar and bicarbonate of soda into a bowl. Add the bran. Cut lard into small pieces and rub into flour until absorbed. Make a well in centre and pour in buttermilk and honey. Beat to make a soft spongy dough. Knead lightly until mixture holds its shape.

Place on a floured baking sheet and bake for 30-35 minutes. Alternatively, shape into two rounds and bake for 25-30 minutes.

Batters

A batter is quite amazingly versatile. The same basic mixture with only a little variation can produce such classics as Crepes Suzette and also Toad in the Hole. It is a most useful extender of meat or vegetables for very little cost as in a Yorkshire Pudding. Used as pancakes it makes a wide variety of sweet and savoury dishes when a range of leftovers from other meals can be used. As a coating for fish or fruit fritters it becomes yet another experience.

Batter at its simplest is a mixture of flour and milk or water. While mixing the ingredients it is well beaten, and this incorporates air into the mixture. The most usual and widely known batters are probably for pancakes or Yorkshire puddings, in which egg and sometimes oil are used. In this case plain flour can be used as the air is sufficiently incorporated by the beating and the addition of egg. For a very plain coating batter however, for example for fried fish, it is only necessary to use flour and water, in which case as the egg is absent, self raising flour is used instead. Once made, a batter should be used fairly promptly, although it can stand for a few minutes to allow the starch grains to expand. By cooking the batter soon after being beaten, the air you have incorporated expands during the cooking, thus making the mixture lighter.

Basic Coating Batter (1)

> *50g (2 oz) self raising flour*
> *2.5ml (½ teaspoon) salt*
> *60ml (4 tablespoons) water*

Sift the flour and salt and mix in the water gradually beating well all the time. The mixture should coat the back of a spoon.

Coat the fish so that it is well sealed and fry immediately in hot fat.

Basic Coating Batter (2)
This is a more elaborate batter and can be used for fritters where a light crisp coating is required.

100g (4 oz) plain flour
5ml (1 teaspoon) salt
5g (¼ oz) fresh yeast
30ml (2 tablespoons) warm water
125ml (¼ pt) LESS 30ml (2 tablespoons) beer or use all water
15ml (1 tablespoon) vegetable oil

Sieve the flour and salt into a warm bowl. Mix yeast with the warm water, work to a cream then with the beer or remaining water and the oil, beat into the flour gradually until a smooth creamlike consistency is obtained. Leave in a warm place for 30-40 minutes.

The batter will have risen a little at this time. When coating, it is essential to cover completely and to fry in hot oil — 175°C (340°F). Drain fritter or whatever thoroughly before serving by removing from the frying pan on to absorbent kitchen paper before transferring to the serving dish.

Pancake Batter

> *100g (4 oz) plain flour*
> *5ml (1 teaspoon) salt*
> *1 egg*
> *250ml (½ pt) milk*
> *15ml (1 tablespoon) vegetable oil*

Sift the flour and salt into a bowl. Make a well in the centre so that you can see the bowl, then break into it the egg. Add a tiny drop of milk and start, very gradually, to stir drawing in the flour little by little, and adding more milk slowly. Once the flour is absorbed in the liquid you can begin to beat more firmly. Add the oil, beat again until the oil has blended. Fry the pancakes this way:

Use a sturdy based frying pan that has been wiped clean and has no residue from anything previously cooked. If in doubt, wipe out the pan with salt on a piece of kitchen paper. Remove all salt. Then pour in about 30ml (2 tablespoons) good quality vegetable oil in the pan and heat. Pour it into another container and keep it by you. Heat the frying pan for a few minutes so that it is really hot. Pour in the oil again, then pour it back into the container. This gives sufficient oil for the pancake. Coat the pan with a very thin layer of the batter. Turn the pan as you put in the batter so that it is really spread thinly. Cook gently until lightly brown, then use a spatula to turn the pancake on to the other side. It's fun to toss the pancake instead of using a spatula, i.e. a quick flick of the wrist so that the pancake leaps into the air and returns to the pan on the other side. Do it by all means if you wish but you'll find a spatula a good deal safer!

If the pancakes are to be eaten there and then you can keep them hot in a dish over a saucepan of hot water and covered with a lid. Serve them with fresh lemon juice and caster sugar.

Yorkshire Pudding

Yorkshire pudding is made from the same basic pancake batter, though personally I use a little less milk so that the consistency is somewhat thicker.

It is traditionally served with roast beef, and if you can cook it in the fat in which the beef is cooking, so much the better, as the delicious flavour is absorbed into the batter. Failing that use a *tin*, not anything else, or it won't be crisp underneath. Melt the dripping in the tin — about 50g (2 oz) and make sure it is really hot before you pour in the batter. Choose a tin that will allow the batter to be about 1cm (¼ in) thick and sufficiently deep for it to rise.

Cook in the middle of a moderately hot oven, 190°C (375°F)/Gas 5, for 15-20 minutes until it is set. For the last 15 minutes put it to the top of the oven to make it rise well and brown. Cut into slices.

Cheesy Herb Popovers

These make an unusual first course or a light supper dish

> *Yorkshire pudding batter described above*
> *75g (3 oz) lard*
> *2 medium onions*
> *75g (3 oz) finely grated Cheddar cheese*
> *5ml (1 teaspoon) dried thyme*
> *5ml (1 teaspoon) dried sage*
> *salt and pepper*

Have ready the batter. Preheat oven to 190°C (375°F)/Gas 5. Chop onion finely, and sauté in 25g (1 oz) of the lard until soft but not browned. Heat remaining lard in a tin, about 25 by 30cm (10 x 12 in). Stir the onions, cheese, dried herbs and seasoning into the batter, pour into the hot fat and cook for 15 minutes in centre of oven, then remaining 20 minutes at the top. Cut into squares and serve with slices of tomato and a green salad.

Fillings for Pancakes
By adding various fillings to pancakes they can make a variety of substantial or lighter supper dishes. The pancakes can be made in advance and layered individually between sheets of greaseproof paper and stored in a refrigerator.

Spinach and Cheese
Try freshly cooked chopped spinach sprinkled with grated nutmeg topped with cheese sauce.

Layer the pancakes and spinach as you would a layer cake, ending with a pancake. Make a thick cheese sauce and spoon over the top. Cover with greased, greaseproof paper and reheat in a moderate oven for 15-20 minutes. Sprinkle a little extra cheese on top and carefully brown under the grill before serving. Cut in wedges as you would a cake.

Chicken and Ham with a Tomato Sauce
Flake leftover chicken and ham and mix together, season well. Layer the pancakes as described before, and top with a thick tomato sauce. Reheat as described for Spinach and Cheese.

Red Cabbage with Apple and Raisins
Cook the cabbage beforehand — it tastes better the next day. Shred red cabbage coarsely and layer up in a casserole with peeled sliced and cored cooking apples, a handful of raisins, chopped onion. Add a tablespoon brown sugar and one of cider vinegar with a little stock to moisten rather than water it. Season well and cook in a tightly fitting casserole for about 1½ hours. Use it to layer up the pancakes. Top with a tomato sauce and reheat as described before.

Smoked Haddock
Cook 450g (1 lb) smoked haddock and add it to a carton soured cream, season with salt and black pepper. Spread it over the pancakes then roll them up and cover with parsley sauce made with 25g (1 oz) butter 25g (1 oz) flour, 250ml (½ pt) milk and 15ml (2 tablespoons) chopped parsley. Sprinkle on 15ml (an extra tablespoon) of parsley before serving.

Mushroom and Ham with Tomato Purée and Garlic
Chop 100g (4 oz) mushrooms and mix with 100g (4 oz) ham and
bind with a small can tomato purée. Add 2 cloves of finely chopped
garlic. This can be served with a thick tomato sauce.

Bacon and Kidney
Use four rashers bacon and four kidneys. Chop bacon, then fry, add
chopped kidney and fry in the same fat. Season. Tomato sauce can
be used as a topping.

Apple Pancakes
Use a really thick apple purée mixed with raisins and chopped
almonds. Reheat as described before, then dredge with icing sugar
and grill carefully just before serving.

Banana and Cream Cheese
Mix mashed bananas with cream cheese, demerara sugar and halved,
de-pipped grapes. Dredge with icing sugar as described before.

Left over Pancakes
These can be used rather as noodles. Cut them into ribbons and deep
fry until golden. Drain well and serve as an accompaniment to meat
and vegetable dishes.

Thick Tomato Sauce
For use with pasta or pancakes or anything where a purée type sauce
is needed

> *1 medium onion*
> *25g (1 oz) butter*
> *one 396g (14 oz) can tomatoes*
> *bay leaf*
> *2 cloves garlic (optional)*
> *salt and pepper*
> *2.5ml (½ teaspoon) dried basil*
> *2.5ml (½ teaspoon) arrowroot*

Chop onion finely. Melt butter in a saucepan and fry onion until
soft and golden. Add tomatoes with liquid, mash with a fork, then
add bay leaf, finely chopped garlic, seasoning and basil.

Cook until well blended and it has a 'rich' look. Remove bay leaf.
Mix arrowroot with tablespoon of water, add to pan, stir well.
Reboil, adjust seasoning if necessary and serve.

Toad in the Hole

A good old family meal that children usually enjoy in particular. Add a few mixed herbs to the batter to give an extra taste.

450g (1 lb) sausages
Yorkshire pudding batter made with 100g (4 oz) flour etc

Preheat oven to 190°C (375°F)/Gas 5. Prick sausages and put into a baking tin approximately 25 by 30cm (10 x 12 in). Bake in oven for about 15 minutes. If there isn't much fat from the sausages add some extra and melt it before adding batter. Pour in the batter over the sausages and cook in the middle of the oven for 15-20 minutes, then at top of oven for last 15 minutes so that batter can brown.

Mushroom Fritters

These make an appetizing first course but they are very rich. Serve with a sharp sauce such as Béchamel with chopped gherkins and capers added.

Use button mushrooms, wash them and dry thoroughly using absorbent kitchen paper. Coat in the fritter batter given under Fruit Fritters but omit the icing sugar. Serve on a hot dish with the sauce separately.

Fruit Fritters

Sweet fritters make a popular dessert and a variety of fruits can be used, the most popular being pineapple, apple and banana.

fritter batter
50g (2 oz) plain flour
pinch salt
5ml (1 teaspoon) icing sugar
45ml (3 tablespoons) warm water
10ml (2 teaspoons) vegetable oil
1 egg white from (grade 3) egg

Sift flour and salt into a bowl with the sugar. Mix water and oil together and add gradually to the flour beating well with a wooden spoon so that it is smooth. Whisk egg white until stiff and fold into flour with a metal spoon. Use the batter at once.

To make the fruit fritters, drain the pineapple rings and dry them gently so that no syrup remains. Peel apples and cut into 1.5cm (½ in) slices. Peel bananas and cut in half lengthways.

Have ready a pan of fat heated to 170°C (350°F). Fully coat the fruit in the batter and lower it carefully into the fat using a perforated spoon. Fry until golden and crisp, turning frequently to keep them evenly cooked. Drain on absorbent kitchen paper, dredge with caster sugar and serve at once.

Crepes Suzette
These really are a spectacular end to a meal, and a certain amount of showmanship is needed. Apart from that they are quite easy. You must have wafer thin pancakes — nothing else will do.

8 wafer thin pancakes
25g (1 oz) butter
50g (2 oz) caster sugar
juice of 2 oranges
45ml (3 tablespoons) orange liqueur

Cook the pancakes and keep them hot between two plates over a pan of boiling water.

Melt the butter in a large, clean frying pan. Add sugar and cook very gently until it is a golden brown. Add the orange juice slowly so that the sauce is rich and smooth.

Put a pancake into the sauce then fold it over twice so that it ends up in a fan shape. Move to the side of the pan and add another pancake and do exactly the same.

The purpose is to coat all the pancakes evenly in the juice. Finally pour over the orange liqueur, set it alight and when flaming carry it to the table and serve immediately.

Cookies and biscuits

Cookies and biscuits are grouped in the same way as cakes — rubbed in, creamed and melted methods are used. The difference is in the amount of moisture added and the lower cooking temperature. Soft flours are the best to use — sometimes cornflour or rice flour is added as well.

You only need enough liquid to hold the mixture together. The aim is to make a stiff dough. Sometimes the fat used is sufficient so that no extra liquid is required. The dough should be lightly kneaded so that an even consistency is obtained.

For all biscuits the oven should be thoroughly preheated so that an even temperature is obtained. The object is for the biscuits to dry out rather than bake. Cook biscuits in centre of oven or one rung below. When first removed from the oven the biscuits will be soft. They will crisp up as they cool. If they are very soft and you think they may break up, leave to cool on the baking tray for a few minutes, then transfer to a wire rack until quite cool.

Store in a thoroughly airtight tin.

Currant Treasures

> 150g (6 oz) self raising flour
> pinch salt
> 2.5ml (½ teaspoon) cinnamon
> 75g (3 oz) margarine
> 50g (2 oz) caster sugar
> 50g (2 oz) chopped walnuts
> 75g (3 oz) currants
> 1 (grade 3) egg
> about 45ml (3 tablespoons) milk

Preheat oven to 190°C (375°F)/Gas 5. Sieve flour, salt and cinnamon into a bowl. Rub in margarine until mixture resembles fine

61

breadcrumbs. Stir in caster sugar, chopped walnuts and currants.

Beat egg with milk and add to make a soft but not sticky dough. Grease two baking sheets well and place 15ml amounts (tablespoons) of the mixture on each, leaving space in between to allow for spreading.

Bake for 15-20 minutes. Cool on a wire rack.

Oaty Chocolate Chip Cookies

100g (4 oz) margarine
100g (4 oz) caster sugar
1 (grade 4) egg, beaten
2.5ml (½ teaspoon) vanilla essence
75g (3 oz) plain flour
pinch salt
50g (2 oz) chocolate chips
40g (1½ oz) rolled oats

Preheat oven to 180°C (350°F)/Gas 4. Cream fat and sugar together until light and fluffy. Beat in the egg and vanilla essence. Sieve the flour and salt into the mixture. Add the chocolate chips and rolled oats and gently fold into the mixture. Place 5ml amounts (teaspoonsful) of the mixture onto greased baking trays leaving space in between to allow for spreading. Bake for 12-15 minutes until very lightly browned. Leave on the baking tray for one minute before transferring to a wire rack to cool.

Coconut Crisps

50g (2 oz) butter
50g (2 oz) caster sugar
15ml (1 tablespoon) golden syrup
30ml (2 tablespoons) lemon juice
50g (2 oz) plain flour
25g (1 oz) desiccated coconut

Preheat oven to 180°C (350°F)/Gas 4. Cream the butter and sugar together until light and fluffy. Beat in the golden syrup and lemon juice. Sift the flour and add to the creamed mixture with the desiccated coconut. Mix thoroughly to give a stiff dropping consistency. Place 5ml amounts (teaspoonsful) of the mixture onto greased baking sheets, allowing plenty of space for spreading. Bake for 15-20 minutes until the edges are golden brown and the centres lightly coloured.

Allow to cool on the trays for two minutes before transferring to a wire rack to finish cooling.

Almond Wheels

150g (6 oz) self raising flour
pinch salt
40g (1½ oz) ground almonds
100g (4 oz) soft brown sugar
50g (2 oz) butter or margarine
1 (grade 4) egg, beaten
flaked almonds to decorate

Preheat oven to 180°C (350°F)/Gas 4. Sift flour and salt into a bowl. Add ground almonds and sugar. Rub in the fat. Stir in the beaten egg and mix to a soft dough. Turn onto a floured surface and knead lightly. Shape into a roll 4-5cm (1½-2 in) in diameter. Wrap in greaseproof paper or foil and place in the refrigerator for one hour. Cut into 6mm (¼ in) slices and place on a greased baking sheet allowing space for the biscuits to spread during baking. Lightly press an almond flake into the centre of each. Bake for 15-20 minutes.

Spice Wheels

Make as for Almond Wheels but omit ground almonds and flaked almonds and add 10ml (2 teaspoons) mixed spice and an extra 40g (1½ oz) self raising flour. Shape, chill and bake as above.

Brandy Snaps

75g (3 oz) black treacle
75g (3 oz) soft brown sugar
75g (3 oz) butter
75g (3 oz) plain flour
5ml (1 teaspoon) ground ginger
5ml (1 teaspoon) grated lemon rind

Preheat oven to 160°C (325°F)/Gas 3. Place the treacle, sugar and butter in a saucepan and heat gently until the butter and sugar have melted. Cool slightly. Sift flour and ginger into the mixture with the lemon rind and beat until smooth.

Grease a baking sheet very thoroughly, then put 10ml amounts (dessertspoons) of the mixture on it, leaving a good space in between to allow for spreading. Bake for 7-8 minutes. Leave to cool just a little, then remove from the tin with a sharp palette knife and while still warm roll each biscuit around the handle of a wooden spoon. If the biscuits become brittle before you can finish, return them to the oven for a minute or two.

Allow to cool on a wire rack.

Anzac Biscuits

> *50g (2 oz) plain flour*
> *50g (2 oz) rolled oats*
> *25g (1 oz) desiccated coconut*
> *100g (4 oz) caster sugar*
> *50g (2 oz) butter or margarine*
> *7.5ml (1½ teaspoons) golden syrup*
> *2.5ml (½ teaspoon) bicarbonate of soda*
> *15ml (1 tablespoon) boiling water*

Preheat oven to 160°C (325°F)/Gas 3. Mix flour, rolled oats, coconut and sugar together in a bowl. Gently warm the butter or margarine and golden syrup in a pan over a low heat until they are evenly blended. Mix the bicarbonate of soda with the boiling water and stir into the melted mixture. Pour the liquid into the dry ingredients and mix well. Roll 5ml amounts (teaspoonsful) of the mixture into small balls and place on greased baking trays leaving plenty of space for the biscuits to spread during baking. Bake in centre of oven for 15 minutes. Transfer to a wire rack to cool.

Crumble Shortbread

> *100g (4 oz) plain flour*
> *50g (2 oz) rice flour or cornflour*
> *50g (2 oz) caster sugar*
> *100g (4 oz) butter or margarine*

For the decoration:

> *15g (½ oz) caster sugar OR*
> *15g (½ oz) almonds finely chopped*

Preheat oven to 160°C (350°F)/Gas 3. Place flour and rice flour, fat and 50g (2 oz) of the caster sugar into a bowl. Rub in the fat until the mixture resembles fine breadcrumbs. Gently squeeze and knead mixture to form a dough. Place a fluted 17.5cm (7 in) flan ring onto a greased baking tray. Turn the dough into the ring and gently flatten the dough to fit the ring. Prick shortbread all over with a fork. Sprinkle 15g (½ oz) caster sugar or the finely chopped almonds on top of the shortbread and press in lightly. Bake in a warm oven for 45 minutes or until firm and light gold in colour. While still warm, mark into wedges using a sharp knife.

Coffee and Walnut Cookies

> *100g (4 oz) butter*
> *50g (2 oz) caster sugar*
> *5ml (1 teaspoon) instant coffee dissolved in*
> *5ml (1 teaspoon) hot water*
> *100g (4 oz) plain flour*
> *50g (2 oz) walnuts, chopped*

Preheat oven to 190°C (375°F)/Gas 5. Cream the butter and sugar together until light and fluffy. Stir in the liquid coffee, flour and walnuts. Drop 5ml amounts (teaspoonsful) of mixture onto a greased baking tray leaving space for the mixture to spread during cooking. Bake for 15-20 minutes until firm to the touch. Leave on tray for one to two minutes before transferring to a wire rack.

Cherry Whirls

> *150g (6 oz) self raising flour*
> *25g (1 oz) caster sugar*
> *75g (3 oz) butter or margarine*
> *1 (grade 4) egg, beaten*

For the filling:

> *50g (2 oz) glacé cherries, chopped*
> *50g (2 oz) soft brown sugar*
> *25g (1 oz) desiccated coconut*
> *25g (1 oz) mixed peel*
> *1 egg yolk*

For the decoration:

> *100g (4 oz) icing sugar, sifted*
> *15ml (1 tablespoon) water*

Preheat oven to 200°C (400°F)/Gas 6. Sift flour into a bowl, add sugar and rub in the fat. Stir in the beaten egg and mix to a soft dough. Turn onto a floured surface, knead lightly and roll out to an oblong 17.5 by 12.5cm (7 x 5 in) with the long edge nearest to you. Mix the filling ingredients together and spread evenly over the dough. Brush one long edge with water and roll up the dough towards this. Cut into 6mm (¼ in) slices. Transfer to a greased baking sheet and bake for 15 minutes. Transfer to a wire rack to cool.

To decorate, mix icing sugar and water to a smooth paste. Pour into a small greaseproof piping bag. Make a small hole in the tip and drizzle a thin strand of icing back and forth across the top of each biscuit.

Chocolate Cherry Stars

> 100g (4 oz) butter or margarine
> 40g (1½ oz) icing sugar, sifted
> 75g (3 oz) plain flour
> 25g (1 oz) cornflour
> 15ml (1 tablespoon) cocoa
> 25g (1 oz) glacé cherries

Preheat oven to 190°C (375°F)/Gas 5. Cream the fat and sugar together until light and fluffy. Sieve together the flour cornflour and cocoa and fold into the creamed mixture. Turn mixture into a forcing bag fitted with a star nozzle and pipe star shapes onto a baking tray. Cut cherries into quarters and press one piece into the centre of each star. Bake in centre of oven for 10-15 minutes. Transfer onto a wire rack to cool.

Viennese Fingers

> 100g (4 oz) butter or margarine
> 40g (1½ oz) icing sugar, sifted
> 2.5ml (½ teaspoon) vanilla essence
> 90g (3½ oz) plain flour, sifted
> 25g (1 oz) cornflour

For the decoration:

> 25g (1 oz) plain chocolate

Preheat oven to 190°C (375°F)/Gas 5. Cream the fat, sugar and essence together until light and fluffy. Gently fold in the sifted flour and cornflour. Turn the mixture into a forcing bag fitted with a star

66

nozzle. Pipe into strips 7.5cm (3 in) long. Bake for 15-20 minutes or until lightly coloured. Transfer onto a wire rack to cool.

To decorate, melt the chocolate in a bowl over a pan of boiling water. Coat both ends of each biscuit with chocolate.

Gypsy Creams

50g (2 oz) margarine
25g (1 oz) lard
45ml (3 tablespoons) golden syrup
150g (6 oz) self raising flour
20ml (4 teaspoons) cocoa
50g (2 oz) caster sugar
50g (2 oz) rolled oats

For the butter cream filling:

50g (2 oz) margarine
100g (4 oz) icing sugar
30ml (2 tablespoons) cocoa
approx 10ml (2 teaspoons) milk

Preheat oven to 160°C (325°F)/Gas 3. Warm together the fats and syrup until liquid. Sift together the flour and cocoa. Place all the ingredients in a bowl and mix together well. Roll pieces of dough about the size of a walnut into balls. Place on a greased baking tray and flatten each ball with a fork. Bake in a warm oven for 20 minutes. Cool on trays. To make the butter cream filling, sift together the icing sugar and cocoa. Cream the ingredients together until smooth, using enough milk to give a firm icing. Use it to sandwich together pairs of the cooled biscuits.

Gingerbread Men

50g (2 oz) margarine
50g (2 oz) caster sugar
15ml (1 tablespoon) golden syrup
100g (4 oz) self raising flour
5ml (1 teaspoon) ground ginger
2.5ml (½ teaspoon) mixed spice
approx 10ml (2 teaspoons) milk
few currants

Preheat oven to 180°C (350°F)/Gas 4. Cream together the fat,

67

sugar and syrup. Sift together the flour and spices and work into the creamed mixture using a fork. Mix in enough milk to make a firm dough. Turn the dough onto a lightly floured surface and knead until smooth. Roll the dough out thinly and cut out gingerbread men using a special cutter or cut around a cardboard shape. Place the men on greased baking sheets and press in currants for eyes. Bake in centre of oven for 10-15 minutes. Cool on baking tray for a few minutes before transferring to a wire rack.

Cornish Fairings

50g (2 oz) caster sugar
50g (2 oz) butter or margarine
50g (2 oz) golden syrup
100g (4 oz) plain flour
5ml (1 teaspoon) ground ginger
7.5ml (1½ teaspoons) baking powder

Preheat oven to 180°C (350°F)/Gas 4. Cream together the sugar, fat and syrup. Sift the flour, ginger and baking powder into the mixture and work together using a fork. The mixture is quite dry and only just binds together. Roll pieces of the dough, the size of a walnut, into balls and place well apart on greased baking trays. Bake for 10-15 minutes until golden brown. Leave on the baking tray to cool before transferring to a wire rack.

Wheatmeal Cheese and Peanut Shorties

50g (2 oz) plain flour
50g (2 oz) wholemeal flour
75g (3 oz) soft margarine
50g (2 oz) finely grated cheese
pinch salt
pinch cayenne pepper
50g (2 oz) salted peanuts, roughly chopped

Preheat oven to 180°C (350°F)/Gas 4. Place all the ingredients except the peanuts in a bowl and work it all together using your hands until smooth. Roll out or press the dough into a 28 by 17.5cm (11 x 7 in) oblong tin. Sprinkle the nuts onto the dough and press well in. Bake in centre of oven for 20 minutes. While still warm mark or cut into fingers or squares.

Lemon Delights

100g (4 oz) butter or margarine
25g (1 oz) icing sugar, sifted
150g (6 oz) plain flour
grated rind of 1 lemon

For the icing:

100g (4 oz) icing sugar, sifted
30ml (2 tablespoons) lemon juice

Preheat oven to 180°C (350°F)/Gas 4. Cream the butter or margarine until light and fluffy. Add the icing sugar and beat well. Fold in the sifted flour and lemon rind. Form into a soft dough. Turn onto a lightly floured surface and roll out the dough to 6mm (¼ in) thick. Cut into biscuits using a 2.5cm (1 in) round cutter. Place onto greased baking trays. Bake for ten minutes until pale gold in colour. Transfer to cool on a wire rack.

For the icing, blend the icing sugar and lemon juice to give a stiff consistency. Thinly coat the surface of each biscuit with the icing.

Currant Circles

100g (4 oz) butter or margarine
25g (1 oz) icing sugar, sifted
150g (6 oz) plain flour
50g (2 oz) currants
50g (2 oz) granulated sugar

Follow same method as for Lemon Delights but omit grated lemon rind and add currants instead. Roll out dough as before. Sprinkle with granulated sugar and roll in lightly. Cut out and bake as for Lemon Delights.

Chocolate and Cherry Cookies

These will never stay around long enough to admire and the chewy taste is very pleasant. Replace cherries and chocolate chips with chopped nuts or raisins if you prefer.

100g (4 oz) margarine
100g (4 oz) soft brown sugar
1 (grade 2) egg
few drops peppermint essence

15ml (1 tablespoon) clear honey
50g (2 oz) chopped glacé cherries
200g (8 oz) self raising flour
50g (2 oz) chocolate polka dots

Cream margarine and sugar together until light and fluffy. Beat egg until yolk and white are blended and gradually add to the margarine mixture. Add the peppermint essence and honey. Roll the chopped glacé cherries in the flour. Sieve remaining flour into the mixture and mix to form a soft dough, then add cherries and chocolate polka dots.

Grease and flour two baking trays. Preheat oven to 180°C (350°F)/Gas 4. Put 10ml amounts (dessertspoons) of the mixture onto the baking tray leaving about 2.5cm (1 in) space between each. Bake in centre of oven for about 12-15 minutes. Leave to cool before turning onto a wire rack.

The art of making cakes — rubbed in, creamed, melted fat methods, sponges, quick mix cakes

Cakes basically fall into three categories as far as the making of them is concerned. These are: rubbed in, cream and melted fat methods. A plain cake is one which has less than half fat to flour, and tea breads fall into this category as well. Rich cakes have more than half fat to flour. The flavourings and fruits added do not make the cake plain or rich — only the proportion of fat to flour, so a fruit cake can be plain and a plain looking cake such as Madeira is termed rich. Don't be confused. It doesn't even matter really, as they all taste marvellous in their own way. In plain cakes the fat is usually rubbed into the flour, and for rich mixtures the fat and sugar is creamed first before flour is added, as it would be difficult to mix more than half fat to flour without becoming rather sticky in the process. In the third category the fats are melted usually with other ingredients such as treacle or sugar. This is the method used for gingerbread, malt breads etc and the proportion of fat to flour is usually about one third. The texture is usually rather more coarse and open than other cake mixtures, and as a rule they keep quite well, and even improve in flavour if kept in an air-tight tin. The softer flours are most usually used for cake making rather than the strong flours. Margarine or butter is used generally for rubbed in and creamed cakes, although lard is often used for the melted method.

Rubbed in mixtures
The fat is rubbed lightly into the flour with the fingertips and thumb as in mixing pastry. Don't rub too hard, just let the flour and fat come into contact with your fingers then drop it and pick up some more. When sufficiently integrated the mixture will look like fine bread-crumbs. This can be done by mechanical mixer, but make sure you

71

don't over mix. Use eggs at room temperature, never straight from the fridge. Rubbed in cakes don't keep as well as the creamed mixtures because of the proportion of fat to flour. Small cakes should be eaten quickly and larger cakes will keep in an airtight tin for about a week.

Creamed mixtures
Creamed mixtures produce a richer cake and because the proportion of fat to flour is too high for mixing by hand they can be mixed with a wooden spoon or by a mixer. The fat should be at room temperature or slightly softer before you start, and when the eggs are introduced to the mixture they should be at room temperature as well. Beat the fat in a warmed bowl with a wooden spoon until it is broken down then add the sugar and continue beating until the fat has paled in colour and has a fluffy appearance. This is the most important part of the operation because the air is incorporated at this stage and the lightness of the cake is determined at this point. Add the eggs, lightly beaten, a little at a time — if they are the same temperature as the fat no curdling should occur. Fold in the flour with a metal spoon so that you retain as much air in the mixture as possible. Bake in the centre of the oven as described in the individual recipes.

Battenburg Cake

> *100g (4 oz) butter or margarine*
> *100g (4 oz) caster sugar*
> *2 eggs, beaten*
> *75g (3 oz) self-raising flour*
> *25g (1 oz) ground almonds*
> *2-3 drops pink colouring*
> *30ml (2 tablespoons) sieved apricot jam*
> *200g (½ lb) marzipan*
> *caster sugar*

Preheat oven to 190°C (375°F)/Gas 5. Grease and line a 17.5cm (7 in) square tin. Divide it in half by placing a 'wall' of double thickness greaseproof paper down the centre. Cream the fat and the sugar together until light and fluffy. Gradually add the eggs a little at a time, beating well after each addition. Lightly fold in the flour and ground almonds using a metal spoon. Turn half the mixture into one side of the tin. Add 2-3 drops of pink colouring to the remaining mixture and stir gently until evenly blended. Spoon into the second half of the tin. Bake in the centre of a moderately hot oven, 190°C (375°F)/Gas 5 for 30 minutes or until firm to the touch. Cool on a wire rack. When cakes are cold, trim the edges and cut each piece in half lengthwise. Spread the sides of the strips with jam and stick them together, alternating the colours. Press the pieces well together then coat the whole of the outside of the cake with jam. Roll out the marzipan thinly in caster sugar to form an oblong 16cm by 30cm (6 in x 12 in). Wrap the marzipan around the cake and pinch with the thumb and forefinger along the outer edges. Trim the edges and score the top of the cake with a sharp knife to give a criss-cross pattern. Sprinkle with caster sugar and press lightly into marzipan.

Coffee and Walnut Ring Cake

> *100g (4 oz) butter or margarine*
> *100g (4 oz) caster sugar*
> *2 eggs, beaten*
> *100g (4 oz) self-raising flour*
> *50g (2 oz) walnuts, chopped*
> *10ml (2 teaspoons) instant coffee*
> *15ml (1 tablespoon) hot water*

For the decoration:

> *100g (4 oz) icing sugar*
> *20ml (4 teaspoons) water*
> *sugar coffee beans*
> *angelica*

Preheat oven to 180°C (350°F)/Gas 4. Cream fat and sugar together until light and fluffy. Gradually add the eggs a little at a time beating well after each addition. Lightly fold in the flour and chopped walnuts. Mix the instant coffee with the hot water and stir gently into the mixture until evenly blended. Spoon into a well greased 20cm (8 in) ring mould and bake in a moderate oven, 180°C (350°F)/Gas 4, for 30 to 35 minutes until firm to the touch. Turn onto a wire rack to cool. For the decoration, mix the icing sugar with the water to form a smooth icing. Pour over top of ring and decorate with sugar coffee beans and angelica.

73

Cherry Cake

150g (6 oz) plain flour
2.5ml (½ teaspoon) baking powder
a pinch of salt
50g (2 oz) ground almonds
125g (5 oz) glacé cherries, quartered
150g (6 oz) butter or margarine
150g (6 oz) caster sugar
2 eggs
30ml (2 tablespoons) milk

Preheat oven to 180°C (350°F)/Gas 4. Sift together the flour, baking powder and salt. Stir in the ground almonds and cherries. Cream together the fat and sugar until light and fluffy. Beat in the eggs one at a time. Fold in the flour mixture and milk. Spoon into a greased and lined 17.5cm (7 in) diameter deep cake tin. Bake in a moderate oven, 180°C (350°F)/Gas 4, for one hour. Cool in the tin for ten minutes before turning out onto a cooling tray.

Mincemeat and Almond Slice

75g (3 oz) wholemeal flour
50g (2 oz) plain flour
25g (1 oz) caster sugar
75g (3 oz) margarine

For the topping:

50g (2 oz) soft margarine
50g (2 oz) caster sugar
1 egg
125g (5 oz) mincemeat
25g (1 oz) self-raising flour
25g (1 oz) ground almonds
few drops almond essence
15g (½ oz) flaked almonds

Preheat oven to 190°C (375°F)/Gas 5. To make the base, place the flours and sugar in a bowl and rub in the fat. Press the mixture firmly into the base of a greased 20cm (8 in) square shallow tin. To make the topping, place the fat, sugar, egg, mincemeat, flour, ground almonds and essence in a bowl and beat well. Spoon on top of the base. Sprinkle on the flaked almonds. Bake in a moderately hot oven, 190°C (375°F)/Gas 5, for 30-35 minutes or until firm.

Apricot Streusal Cake

> *150g (6 oz) self-raising flour*
> *pinch of salt*
> *75g (3 oz) margarine*
> *50g (2 oz) caster sugar*
> *75g (3 oz) dried apricots, chopped*
> *grated rind and juice of ½ orange*
> *1 egg beaten*
> *milk to mix*

For the streusal topping:

> *25g (1 oz) butter*
> *60ml (4 tablespoons) plain flour*
> *15ml (1 tablespoon) sugar*

Preheat oven to 190°C (375°F)/Gas 5. Sift together the flour and salt. Rub in the fat. Stir in the remaining ingredients to make a soft dropping consistency. Spoon into a greased 450g (1 lb) small loaf tin. To make the streusal topping melt the butter and stir in the flour and sugar. Sprinkle over the top of the cake. Bake in a moderately hot oven, 190°C (375°F)/Gas 5, for 35-40 minutes.

Wholemeal Sultana Cake

> *200g (8 oz) wholemeal flour*
> *pinch of salt*
> *10ml (2 teaspoons) baking powder*
> *5ml (1 teaspoon) mixed spice*
> *100g (4 oz) margarine*
> *75g (3 oz) demerara sugar*
> *100g (4 oz) sultanas*
> *2 eggs, beaten*
> *milk to mix*

Preheat oven to 190°C (375°F)/Gas 5. Place the flour, salt, baking powder and spice in a bowl. Rub in the fat. Stir in the sugar, sultanas, eggs and enough milk to make a dropping consistency. Place in a greased and lined 15cm (6 in) square deep cake tin. Bake in a moderately hot oven, 190°C (375°F)/Gas 5 for 50 minutes.

Coconut and Orange Iced Cake

200g (8 oz) self-raising flour
pinch of salt
150g (6 oz) caster sugar
100g (4 oz) desiccated coconut
150g (6 oz) butter or margarine
grated rind of 1 orange (reserve juice)
1 egg beaten plus milk to make up to 125ml (¼ pt)

For the decoration:

100g (4 oz) icing sugar
20ml (4 teaspoons) orange juice
25g (1 oz) shredded coconut
8 orange jelly sweets

Preheat oven to 180°C (350°F)/Gas 4. Sift flour and salt into a large mixing bowl. Add the sugar and coconut and rub in the fat until mixture resembles fine breadcrumbs. Stir in orange rind, egg and milk. Beat mixture to form a smooth dropping consistency. Spoon into a greased and lined 17.5cm (7 in) round cake tin. Bake in a moderate oven, 180°C (350°F)/Gas 4, for 50-60 minutes or until firm to touch and a skewer comes out clean. Turn onto a wire rack to cool. To decorate, mix icing sugar with orange juice to form a smooth icing. Spread over top of cake. Decorate with shredded coconut and orange jelly sweets.

Rich Fruit Cake

75g (3 oz) lard
75g (3 oz) margarine
150g (6 oz) soft brown sugar
15ml (1 tablespoon) black treacle
200g (8 oz) plain flour
5ml (1 teaspoon) powdered ginger
5ml (1 teaspoon) mixed spice
3 large eggs
400g (1 lb) mixed dried fruit

blended. Sift flour, ginger and mixed spice. Beat eggs into fat mixture one at a time with 15ml (a tablespoon) of the flour to prevent curdling. Mix in dried fruit then flour and spices. Well grease and line a 900g (2 lb) loaf tin or line with foil. Pour in mixture and smooth top. Bake in centre of low oven 150°C (300°F)/Gas 2 for 2¼ hours. Test it is cooked by putting a skewer down centre of cake. It should come out quite clean. Cool in tin, then turn out onto a wire rack.

Cardamon Cake

>300g (12 oz) self-raising flour
>5ml (1 teaspoon) baking powder
>100g (4 oz) butter or margarine
>175g (7 oz) granulated sugar
>15ml (1 tablespoon) ground cardamon
>125g (5 fl oz) single cream
>75ml (3 fl oz) milk

>For the topping:

>>25g (1 oz) flaked almonds
>>25g (1 oz) granulated sugar
>>10ml (2 teaspoons) cinnamon

Preheat oven to 200°C (400°F)/Gas 6. Sift flour and baking powder in a large bowl. Rub in the fat until the mixture resembles fine breadcrumbs. Mix in the sugar and the cardamon. Add the cream and milk and stir well until a soft dough is formed. Turn the mixture into a greased and lined large loaf tin. Level the surface and sprinkle evenly with the topping. Bake at 200°C (400°F)/Gas 6 for one hour or until firm to the touch. Turn out of tin and place on a wire rack to cool.

Honey Sponge Gateau

>For the sponge:

>>100g (4 oz) butter or margarine
>>100g (4 oz) caster sugar
>>10ml (rounded dessertspoon) clear honey
>>2 (grade 2) eggs
>>2.5ml (½ teaspoon) vanilla flavouring
>>200g (8 oz) self-raising flour
>>2.5ml (½ level teaspoon) baking powder
>>75g (3 oz) sifted icing sugar
>>90ml (6 tablespoons) milk
>>50g (2 oz) chopped hazel nuts

For the butter cream:

50g (2 oz) unsalted butter
100g (4 oz) sifted icing sugar
5ml (1 rounded teaspoon) clear honey

For the glacé icing:

100g (4 oz) sieved icing sugar
15ml (1 tablespoon) warm water
5ml (1 teaspoon) clear honey
whole hazel nuts to decorate

Cut up fat and beat until soft. Add caster sugar and honey and beat until light and creamy and the mixture has lost any 'gritty' feel. Whisk eggs and vanilla lightly then add to butter mixture. Sift flour, baking powder and icing sugar and add gradually to the mix, adding milk halfway through to prevent mixture getting too stiff. Finally add the chopped hazelnuts.

Grease two 17.5cm (7 in) sandwich tins and divide the mixture equally. Preheat oven to 180°C (350°F)/Gas 4 and cook just above centre of oven for about 20 minutes. Turn out onto a wire rack and allow to cool. This amount makes two large sandwich cakes. You can if you wish, cut one sandwich cake in half and use the following butter cream and glacé icing on one cake only, or double butter cream quantities to make an even larger cake. However, the cakes are beautifully moist and the quantities as described make a delicious 'Sunday' tea gateau.

To make the butter cream, beat butter and gradually work in icing sugar. Add clear honey. Sandwich the two cakes together.

To make the glacé icing, sieve the icing sugar into a bowl. Dissolve the honey in the warm water then gradually beat into icing sugar. Pour over the top of the cake and allow to set. Add toasted hazelnuts as decoration.

Apple Cheesecake

200g (8 oz) plain flour
10ml (2 level teaspoons) baking powder
5ml (1 level teaspoon) cinnamon
75g (3 oz) butter
50g (2 oz) caster sugar
1 (grade 2) egg

78

For the filling:

450g (1 lb) cooking apples
1, 225g (8 oz) pack soft cream cheese
75g (3 oz) caster sugar
25g (1 oz) flour
15ml (1 tablespoon) milk
50g (2 oz) sultanas

Preheat oven to 180°C (350°F)/Gas 4. Sieve flour, baking powder and cinnamon into a bowl. Rub in the butter until mixture resembles fine breadcrumbs. Stir in the caster sugar. Beat egg until yolk and white are blended then add to the dry mix. It will be a crumbly mix at this stage. Grease a 20cm (8 in) loose bottomed cake tin and press the mixture firmly on the bottom. Peel, core and cut the apples into thin slices. Arrange over top of cake mixture. Sprinkle over 25g (1 oz) caster sugar, leaving the remainder for the topping. To make the topping, cream cheese with a wooden spoon until soft. Beat in the remaining caster sugar with the flour and the milk. Add sultanas. Spread over apple mixture. Cover with buttered greaseproof paper and cook for about 45 minutes. Serve hot or cold.

Devil's Food Cake

This is quite a light chocolate cake and although it uses real chocolate, it is economical on eggs, which evens out the cost a bit.

200g (8 oz) self-raising flour
5ml (1 level teaspoon) ground cinnamon
2.5ml (½ teaspoon) ground nutmeg
2.5ml (½ level teaspoon) bicarbonate of soda
75g (3 oz) plain chocolate
125ml (¼ pt) milk
100g (4 oz) butter
200g (8 oz) caster sugar
2 (grade 2) eggs
5ml (1 teaspoon) vanilla essence

For the butter icing:

150g (6 oz) butter
225g (9 oz) icing sugar
5ml (1 teaspoon) vanilla essence
15-30ml (between 1 and 2 tablespoons) milk

79

Preheat oven to 180°C (350°F)/Gas 4. Sieve flour, spices and bicarbonate of soda on to a plate or sheet of greaseproof paper. Break chocolate up into pieces and put in a basin with the milk. Put basin in a pan of hot water over a low heat until chocolate has melted and blended with the milk. Cream butter and caster sugar until light and creamy in colour and the sugar has lost its gritty taste. Beat eggs with vanilla essence and then gradually mix into the creamed mixture adding 15ml (a tablespoon) of flour with each addition. Stir in the chocolate milk alternately with the remaining flour and mix until smooth. Grease two 20cm (8 in) sandwich tins and pour in the mixture equally between the two. Bake just above centre of oven for about 35-40 minutes. Turn out and cool on a wire rack.

To make the butter icing, cream butter then gradually add the sieved icing sugar, vanilla essence and enough milk to make a stiff, spreading consistency. Spread half the mixture onto the cakes to sandwich them together, then spread the other half over the top. Finish off by gently 'swirling' the butter icing with a fork to give a ridged effect.

Mixed Spice Yoghourt Cake
An unusual highly spiced cake that's not as sweet as most cakes, so it may well appeal more to the non-sweet-tooth brigade.

> *100g (4 oz) butter*
> *300g (12 oz) caster sugar*
> *300g (12 oz) self-raising flour*
> *5ml (1 teaspoon) baking powder*
> *5ml (1 teaspoon) bicarbonate of soda*
> *1ml (¼ teaspoon) salt*
> *2.5ml (½ teaspoon) ground nutmeg*
> *5ml (1 teaspoon) cinnamon*
> *2.5ml (½ teaspoon) mixed spice*
> *3 large eggs*
> *125ml (¼ pt) plain yoghourt*

For the topping:

> *25g (1 oz) desiccated coconut*
> *25g (1 oz) chopped walnuts*
> *25g (1 oz) soft brown sugar*
> *45ml (3 tablespoons) double cream*

Heat oven to 180°C (350°F)/Gas 4. Cream butter and sugar until very well blended. Sift all the dry ingredients. Add eggs to butter mixture one at a time adding 15ml (a tablespoon) of flour with each addition to prevent curdling. Stir rest of dry ingredients into the mixture alternating with the yoghourt. Stir until well blended and smooth. Pour it into a 20cm (8 in) cake tin which has been very well greased. Cook in centre of oven for 55 minutes or until cooked right through to the centre. Turn out on to a wire rack and allow to cool. To make the topping, blend all the ingredients together. Spread over the cake.

Orange Spice Cake

> *100g (4 oz) margarine*
> *150g (6 oz) soft brown sugar*
> *2 (grade 2) eggs*
> *125ml (¼ pt) plain yoghourt*
> *rind and juice of one large orange*
> *100g (4 oz) plain flour*
> *100g (4 oz) wholemeal plain flour*
> *10ml (2 level teaspoons) baking powder*
> *2.5ml (½ level teaspoon) salt*
> *5ml (1 level teaspoon) cinnamon*

Preheat oven to 180°C (350°F)/Gas 4. Grease a 17.5cm (7 in) cake tin. Cream margarine and sugar until soft and fluffy and the sugar has lost its gritty feel. Beat eggs, combine with the yoghourt and blend well in. Add orange rind and juice. Sift flours, baking powder, salt and cinnamon together and add to mixture. Stir with a metal spoon until just blended. Turn into a greased 17.5cm (7 in) cake tin and cook just below centre of oven for one hour. Turn out and cool on a wire rack.

Polka Dot Cake

> *100g (4 oz) margarine*
> *100g (4 oz) caster sugar*
> *3 (grade 3) eggs*
> *200g (8 oz) self-raising flour*
> *30-45ml (2-3 tablespoons) milk*
> *75g (3 oz) chocolate chips*
> *30ml (2 rounded tablespoons) apricot jam*
> *glacé icing made with*
> *100g (4 oz) icing sugar*
> *15ml (1 tablespoon) water*

Preheat oven to 180°C (350°F)/Gas 4. Grease and line a 17.5cm (7 in) cake tin. Cream margarine and sugar together until mixture is light and creamy in colour and has lost its gritty texture. Add eggs, one at a time with 15ml (a tablespoon) of flour. Sieve in remaining flour, and the milk and stir in the chocolate chips. Turn into the cake tin, smooth the top and bake in centre of oven for about one hour 15 minutes. Turn out to cool on a wire rack. Divide cake into two rounds and spread thickly with the jam. Put them together again. Make the icing. Sieve icing sugar into a bowl and beat in the water. Pour over the top of the cake and allow icing to set before serving.

If you are used to making your own yoghourt, it's easy to add it to recipes. It gives an added flavour and can be used in recipes as a substitute to sour milk or buttermilk, in which case add 5ml (a level teaspoon) baking powder.

Spiced Raisin Cake

100g (4 oz) margarine
150g (6 oz) soft brown sugar
100g (4 oz) raisins
125ml (¼ pt) plain yoghourt
2 (grade 2) eggs
200g (8 oz) plain flour
10ml (2 level teaspoons) baking powder
2.5ml (½ teaspoon) salt
5ml (1 level teaspoon) EACH of ground nutmeg, cloves and cinnamon

Preheat oven to 180°C (350°F)/Gas 4. Grease a 17.5cm (7 in) cake tin. Cream margarine and sugar until soft and fluffy. When sufficiently beaten it will be light in texture and non gritty. Stir in raisins. Mix yoghourt with beaten eggs and add to mixture. Sift flour, baking powder and spices. Add to mixture, then fold in lightly with a metal spoon until blended. By blending in lightly you retain the volume of air you have painstakingly beaten in to the mixture earlier on. Transfer mixture to the greased cake tin and bake just below centre of oven for about an hour.

Seed Cake

200g (8 oz) plain flour
pinch salt
10ml (2 teaspoons) baking powder

100g (4 oz) butter
150g (6 oz) sugar
3 medium eggs
10ml (2 teaspoons) caraway seeds

Preheat oven to 180°C (350°F)/Gas 4. Grease a 20cm (8 in) cake tin. Sieve flour, salt and baking powder. Cream butter and sugar together until white and creamy and the butter is no longer gritty. Beat eggs together until white and yolk are blended. Add to creamed mixture a little at a time adding 15ml (a tablespoon) of flour with each addition. Fold in remaining flour and caraway seeds. Add a little milk if necessary to make a soft though firm consistency. Put mixture in greased cake tin and cook in centre of oven at 180°C (350°F)/Gas 4 for 1-1¼ hours.

Rich Chocolate Cake

200g (8 oz) margarine
150g (6 oz) dark brown sugar
150g (6 oz) black treacle
150g (6 oz) self-raising flour
50g (2 oz) cocoa
4 (grade 4) eggs
2.5ml (½ teaspoon) peppermint essence
chocolate butter icing
sprinkling of icing sugar

Preheat oven to 180°C (350°F)/Gas 4. Beat together margarine, sugar and treacle until light and fluffy in texture and sugar is no longer gritty. Sieve together flour and cocoa. Gradually add lightly beaten eggs and essence to margarine mix adding 15ml (a tablespoon) flour with each addition. Fold in remaining flour. Well grease a 20cm (8 in) cake tin and pour in mixture. Bake just below centre of oven for about 45 minutes or until cake shrinks slightly from the sides of the tin. Turn out onto a wire rack and leave to cool. When cold, cut in half, sandwich together with chocolate butter icing (see page 118) and sprinkle icing sugar over the top.

Poppy Seed Cake

25g (1 oz) poppy seeds
125ml (5 fl oz) buttermilk
75g (3 oz) butter

75g (3 oz) lard
250g (10 oz) caster sugar
250g (10 oz) plain flour
10ml (2 teaspoons) baking powder
5ml (1 teaspoon) bicarbonate of soda
3 large eggs
5ml (1 teaspoon) vanilla essence

For the topping:

25g (1 oz) caster sugar
5ml (1 teaspoon) cinnamon
5ml (1 teaspoon) cocoa

Preheat oven to 180°C (350°F)/Gas 4. Stir poppy seeds into buttermilk and leave for at least 20 minutes. Beat butter and lard together until blended. Add sugar and continue beating until sugar has lost its gritty flavour. Sieve flour, baking powder and bicarbonate of soda. Add egg yolks to creamed mixture adding 15ml (a tablespoon) of flour with each one. Add remaining flour, buttermilk and vanilla essence and blend. Whisk egg whites until stiff then fold in to cake mixture. Make topping by blending sugar, cinnamon and cocoa. Turn half into a 20cm (8 in) greased cake tin, then sprinkle over half the topping. Add remaining mixture then sprinkle over remaining topping. Cook at 180°C (350°F)/Gas 4 for 50-60 minutes. Turn out and allow to cool.

Marble Cake
The combination of the different colourings and the marzipan topping makes this a lazy man's Battenburg, and is distinctly easier if you don't want to be too precise.

150g (6 oz) butter
150g (6 oz) caster sugar
150g (6 oz) self raising flour minus 15ml (1 tablespoon)
3 (size 4) standard eggs
1ml (¼ teaspoon) cochineal colouring
15ml (1 tablespoon) cocoa
200g (8 oz) packet of marzipan
30ml (2 tablespoons) apricot jam

Preheat oven to 180°C (350°F)/Gas 4. Grease a 17.5cm (7 in) cake tin. Cream fat to soften, then add sugar and beat until light and fluffy. Sift flour. Add eggs one at a time, together with 15ml (a tablespoon) of the flour to prevent curdling. Add remainder of flour and blend in evenly. Divide mixture into three equal portions and put each one in a separate basin. Colour the first mixture with the cochineal, and the second with the cocoa. Put spoonfuls of each mixture into the cake tin in a random way so that the colours all run together. Smooth the top carefully and bake for 35-40 minutes. Turn out onto a wire rack and allow to cool. Roll out the marzipan carefully into a circle to fit the top of the cake exactly. Brush top of cake with apricot jam and press on the marzipan. Neaten by running a rolling pin vertically around the edge of the marzipan. Leave to dry out and just before serving, brown very carefully under a hot grill.

Honey Plum Sponge
This is the sort of sweet you can serve if you are caught with unexpected guests. Most of us keep a can of plums in the larder, or other canned fruit and this recipe makes a little go a long way.

> 75g (3 oz) butter
> 15ml (1 tablespoon) clear honey
> 1, 538g (1 lb 3 oz) can plums
> 50g (2 oz) caster sugar
> 2 (grade 2) large eggs
> 100g (4 oz) plain flour
> 2.5ml (½ teaspoon) baking powder

Preheat oven to 190°C (375°F)/Gas 5. Take 25g (1 oz) of the butter and melt it in a saucepan. Add honey and stir until blended. Pour into the bottom of a 20cm (8 in) soufflé dish. Drain the plums and reserve the liquid. Discard stones from plums and put the fruit in the bottom of the dish. Take remaining butter and beat to soften it then add caster sugar and beat until light and fluffy. Separate the eggs, add the egg yolks to the butter mixture and fold in the flour which has been sieved with the baking powder. Whisk egg whites until stiff and fold in. Pour over the plums and bake in centre of oven for about 35 minutes. Serve with the heated up juice from the plums.

Date and Walnut Cake

> 200g (8 oz) self raising flour
> 75g (3 oz) butter
> 75g (3 oz) caster sugar
> 75g (3 oz) dates

25g (1 oz) walnuts
1 (grade 3) egg
125ml (¼ pt) approx milk

Preheat oven to 180°C (350°F)/Gas 4. Sift flour into bowl and rub in butter until mixture resembles fine breadcrumbs. Stir in sugar. Stone dates and chop well. Chop walnuts, this is easier if you use a wet knife. Stir into rubbed in mixture. Beat egg and add the milk then stir into flour and mix to a soft but not sticky dough. Transfer to a 17.5cm (7 in) cake tin, smooth the top and bake for about an hour in centre of oven. Cake should be brown and have shrunk very slightly away from the tin. Turn out onto a wire rack and leave to cool.

Plain Cherry Cake

Make as above, but omit dates and walnuts and substitute 75g (3 oz) glacé cherries. Cut cherries into halves or quarters, dust lightly in the *weighed out* flour (not extra flour or you will distort the quantities). Stir in after mixing in the sugar.

Apple Cake

200g (8 oz) self raising flour
75g (3 oz) butter
75g (3 oz) caster sugar
1 large cooking apple, about 150g (6 oz)
50g (2 oz) raisins
1 (size 3) egg
75ml (5-6 tablespoons) milk
extra tablespoon sugar mixed with 5ml (level teaspoon) mixed spice

Preheat oven to 180°C (350°F)/Gas 4. Sift flour into a bowl and rub in butter with the fingertips until mixture resembles fine breadcrumbs. Stir in sugar. Peel and core apple and grate onto a plate. Add to flour mixture together with raisins. Beat egg in a bowl until yolk and white are blended, add milk then stir into mixture. Grease a 1 litre (2 pint) fireproof dish and transfer the mixture, smooth the top with a knife. Sprinkle extra sugar and spice over the top. Cook in centre of oven for about 30 minutes then lower heat to 160°C (350°F)/Gas 3 and cook for a further half hour.

Serve hot with custard or leave to cool and serve as a cake.

Apple and Date Cake

> 300g (12 oz) plain flour
> pinch salt
> 5ml (1 level teaspoon) bicarbonate of soda
> 5ml (1 teaspoon) ground ginger
> 150g (6 oz) butter
> 150g (6 oz) caster sugar
> 150g (6 oz) dates
> 250ml (½ pt) apple purée
> 125ml (¼ pt) or less of milk

Preheat oven to 180°C (350°F)/Gas 4. Sift flour, salt, bicarbonate of soda and ginger into a bowl. Rub in butter until mixture resembles fine breadcrumbs. Stir in caster sugar. Chop dates into small pieces, add to mixture then stir in apple purée and enough milk to make a firm but sticky dough. Transfer to a 17.5cm (7 in) cake tin, spread the top smoothly then bake in centre of oven for about 1¼ hours or until cake is cooked right through. Leave to cool on a wire rack. This cake keeps well and is economical although no eggs are used.

Sherry Fruit Cake

This is a halfway house between a really rich Christmassy type cake and the family fruit cake to eat during the week. The sherry makes it extra special, so hang the expense.

> 150g (6 oz) mixed dried fruit
> 50g (2 oz) dried figs
> miniature bottle cream sherry
> 200g (8 oz) self raising flour
> 100g (4 oz) butter
> 50g (2 oz) dark brown sugar
> 2 (grade 2) eggs

Weigh out dried fruit and put into a bowl. Cut up the dried figs and add to fruit. Pour over sherry, cover with a plate and leave for at least an hour. Preheat oven to 180°C (350°F)/Gas 4. Sift flour into a bowl. Cut up butter and rub in flour until mixture resembles fine breadcrumbs. Stir in sugar. Add dried fruit. Beat eggs together lightly then stir in to make a soft but not sticky dough. Turn into a well greased 17.5cm (7 in) cake tin and bake in centre of oven for about an hour or until cake has shrunk slightly from the sides of the tin. After the first half an hour lower temperature to 160°C (325°F)/Gas 3. Turn out to cool on a wire rack.

No Egg Marmalade Cake

This cake has a beautiful flavour. The extra baking powder and bicarbonate of soda give it the rising quality it needs.

200g (8 oz) flour
10ml (2 level teaspoons) baking powder
5ml (1 level teaspoon) bicarbonate of soda
2.5ml (½ teaspoon) salt
100g (4 oz) butter
100g (4 oz) caster sugar
45ml (3 rounded tablespoons) thick cut marmalade (as much above as below the rim of the spoon)
50g (2 oz) chopped mixed peel
60ml (4 tablespoons) milk to mix

Preheat oven to 180°C (350°F)/Gas 4. Grease a 17.5cm (7 in) cake tin. Sift flour, baking powder, bicarbonate of soda and salt into a bowl. Rub in butter until mixture resembles fine breadcrumbs. Sprinkle in the caster sugar and blend well in. Stir in the marmalade, mixed peel and milk to mix to a stiffish dough. Add a little more milk if necessary. Turn into the greased 17.5cm (7 in) cake tin, smooth the top and bake just below centre of oven for about 55 minutes to one hour. Turn out onto a wire rack and allow to cool.

Lemon Seedcake

A seedcake with a taste of lemon gives an extra zing. Use butter and don't try to substitute margarine — it won't taste the same.

200g (8 oz) self raising flour
100g (4 oz) butter
100g (4 oz) caster sugar
5ml (1 level teaspoon) caraway seeds
grated rind of 1 lemon
2 (grade 2) eggs
30ml (2 tablespoons) milk

Preheat oven to 190°C (375°F)/Gas 5. Sift flour into a bowl and rub in butter until mixture resembles fine breadcrumbs. Stir in sugar, caraway seeds and grated lemon rind. Beat eggs until yolks and whites are blended. Stir into flour mix and add milk to make a soft not sticky dough. Grease a 17.5cm (7 in) cake tin. Transfer cake mixture to tin. Smooth top and bake in centre of oven for about 50 minutes. Turn out onto a wire rack and leave to cool.

Coconut Chocolate Chip Cake

250g (10 oz) plain flour
10ml (2 level teaspoons) baking powder
125g (5 oz) butter
125g (5 oz) caster sugar
65g (2½ oz) desiccated coconut
50g (2 oz) chocolate chips
2 (grade 2) eggs
60ml (4 tablespoons) milk (or enough to make a stiff dough)

Preheat oven to 180°C (350°F)/Gas 4. Sift the flour and baking powder into a bowl. Cut butter into small pieces and rub in with the fingertips until mixture resembles fine breadcrumbs. Sprinkle in the caster sugar. Add coconut and chocolate chips. Add eggs and enough milk to make mixture into a stiff dough. Turn out into a 17.5cm (7 in) cake tin, smooth the top and bake in centre of oven for about 1¼ hours. Turn out to cool on a wire rack.

Lemon Cake
A tangy refreshing taste to a plain cake

200g (8 oz) plain flour
5ml (1 level teaspoon) baking powder
5ml (1 level teaspoon) salt
150g (6 oz) margarine
150g (6 oz) caster sugar
1 large lemon
2 large eggs

Preheat oven to 180°C (350°F)/Gas 4. Well grease a 17.5cm (7 in) cake tin. Sieve flour, baking powder and salt into a bowl. Rub in margarine until mixture resembles fine breadcrumbs. Stir in caster sugar. Grate rind from lemon, then extract the juice. Pour rind and juice into cake mixture. Beat eggs lightly, then stir into the flour and mix until blended. Transfer to cake tin, smooth top of mixture and bake in centre of oven for about 1¼ hours. When quite cool, cover with glacé icing.

89

Orange Cake

Substitute one medium size orange instead of the lemon, but don't use more than 30ml (2 tablespoons) of orange juice.

Lemon or Orange Glacé Icing.

100g (4 oz) icing sugar
15ml (1 tablespoon) orange or lemon juice

Sieve icing sugar and gradually beat in the juice. Pour over the cake and allow to set. In this instance it's a nice idea to let the icing run down the sides of the cake to give a casual touch, and of course, it also adds extra icing to the cut slices.

Honey Ginger

The ginger gives this cake an added spice but it is quite mild.

150g (6 oz) butter
150g (6 oz) caster sugar
15ml (1 rounded tablespoon) honey (as much above as below the
*   rim of the spoon)*
2 large eggs
15ml (1 tablespoon) milk
200g (8 oz) plain flour
10ml (2 teaspoons) baking powder
5ml (1 teaspoon) ground ginger

For the icing:

50g (2 oz) butter
100g (4 oz) icing sugar
15ml (1 tablespoon) honey
few drops milk

To decorate:

thin slices of stem ginger, well drained from the syrup

Preheat oven to 190°C (375°F)/Gas 5. Well grease two 17.5cm (7 in) sandwich tins. Cream butter and sugar by beating with a wooden spoon until mixture is pale and creamy and sugar is no longer gritty. Beat in honey. Sift flour and spices and add with the eggs and milk beating well until blended. Bake in centre of oven for 20 minutes. Allow to cool in tin for a few minutes then transfer to a wire rack to cool. Make butter icing by beating butter to soften, then adding icing sugar, a little at a time. Beat in honey and a few drops of milk to bring icing to a good spreading consistency. Use half icing to sandwich cakes together, then spread remaining icing on top. Decorate with thin slices of stem ginger.

Plum Shortcake

For the shortcake:

200g (8 oz) plain flour
pinch salt
7.5ml (1½ level teaspoons) baking powder
75g (3 oz) butter
25g (1 oz) caster sugar
1 large (grade 2) egg
45ml (3 or 4 tablespoons) milk
15g (½ oz) melted butter

For the filling:

250ml (½ pt) very thick cold custard
30ml (2 or 3 tablespoons) whipped double cream
medium can 400g (14 oz) canned plums

Preheat the oven to 220°C (425°F)/Gas 7. To make the shortcake, sift flour, salt and baking powder into a bowl. Rub in the butter with fingertips until mixture resembles fine breadcrumbs. Stir in the sugar. Mix eggs with milk and pour into centre of the dry ingredients, and mix together to form a soft but not sticky dough. Turn onto a floured board and knead lightly with the fingertips to make a soft, smooth dough. Divide in two. Put each piece of dough into a well greased 20cm (8 in) sandwich tin and press with the palm of the hand to shape it to fit the tin. Brush top with melted butter and cook at just above centre of oven for 20-25 minutes until it is golden brown. Cool on a wire rack. Remove any skin from custard and whip in the cream. Drain the plums reserving the juice. Pierce each shortcake with a fork and carefully spoon over the juice and allow it to soak in. Stone plums, reserving two or three halves to decorate the top. Use the remaining plums and half the custard mixture to sandwich the two cakes together. Spread remaining custard mixture over the top of the cake. Carefully wipe the remaining plum halves with a tissue to remove excess juice, then use them to decorate the top of the cake.

Melted Fat Method

The remaining method of adding fat to flour is the melted fat method, used mainly with gingerbreads, parkin and so on. The average proportion is one third fat to flour. Some recipes don't include eggs. When heating fat and sugar with the syrup, heat it gently only enough to blend the ingredients. When adding eggs to the flour at the same time it is particularly important to see that the mixture is only warm, not hot.

In making gingerbread, bicarbonate of soda is used as the raising agent. This ingredient alone is only used when a strong flavoured mixture, such as gingerbread is made. The harsh flavour is disguised and the yellowing effect adds colour to the finished result. Also, the bicarbonate of soda has a weakening effect on the gluten which makes the finished cake soft and crumbly. Gingerbread can burn around the edges quite easily so use a low oven, grease the tin well, and if the tins you use are thin, tie a piece of brown paper around the outside whilst cooking. Because the batter does not set very quickly at such a low temperature, try not to open the oven door at least during the beginning of the baking. If you do, the cake may sink in the middle. If the tin has been lined remove the paper from the cake while still warm, before leaving to cool on the wire rack. Gingerbread improves if it is kept for 24 hours in an airtight tin before eating.

Sour Cream Gingerbread

> *200g (8 oz) plain flour*
> *5ml (1 teaspoon) bicarbonate of soda*
> *15ml (1 tablespoon) ground ginger*
> *2.5ml (½ teaspoon) salt*
> *100g (4 oz) butter*
> *100g (4 oz) dark brown sugar*
> *45ml (3 rounded tablespoons) black treacle*
> *2 (grade 4) eggs*
> *125ml (5 fl oz) sour cream*

Preheat oven to 150°C (300°F)/Gas 2. Sift flour, soda, ginger and salt together. Over a low heat melt butter, sugar and treacle. Pour slowly into dry mixture and beat until smooth. Add the beaten eggs and sour cream, stirring until well blended. Pour into 20cm (8 in) round tin and bake just below centre of oven for 1¼ hours.

Wholemeal Gingerbread

100g (4 oz) plain flour
5ml (1 teaspoon) bicarbonate of soda
large pinch of salt
10ml (2 teaspoons) cinnamon
10ml (2 teaspoons) ground ginger
100g (4 oz) wholemeal flour
75g (3 oz) soft brown sugar
50g (2 oz) sultanas
50g (2 oz) crystallized ginger, chopped
100g (4 oz) black treacle
100g (4 oz) golden syrup
150g (6 oz) margarine
2 eggs
30ml (2 tablespoons) milk
flaked almonds

Preheat oven to 180°C (350°F)/Gas 4. Sift the plain flour, soda, salt and spices into a bowl. Add the wholemeal flour, sugar, sultanas and ginger. Heat the treacle, syrup and fat together in a pan until melted, and stir into the flour. Beat in the eggs and milk. Pour the mixture into a greased and lined 28 x 18cm (11 x 7 in) tin. Sprinkle on the flaked almonds. Bake for 20 minutes then reduce the heat to 160°C (325°F)/Gas 3 for a further 20 minutes or until firm and springy to touch.

Gingerbread

200g (8 oz) plain flour
5ml (1 teaspoon) mixed spices
15ml (1 tablespoon) ground ginger
5ml (1 teaspoon) bicarbonate of soda
50g (2 oz) sugar
100g (4 oz) margarine
150g (6 oz) black treacle
50g (2 oz) golden syrup
125ml (¼ pt) milk
2 eggs, beaten

Preheat oven to 150°C (300°F)/Gas 2. Sift together the flour, spices and soda. Place the sugar, fat, treacle and syrup into a pan and warm until the fat has melted. Stir the warmed mixture, milk and eggs into the flour. Pour into a greased and lined 900g (2 lb) large loaf tin and bake 1-1¼ hours or until firm.

Quick Lemon Bake

> *150g (6 oz) butter or margarine*
> *250g (10 oz) caster sugar*
> *150g (6 oz) self raising flour*
> *2 eggs, beaten*
> *juice of 1 medium sized lemon*

Preheat oven to 180°C (350°F)/Gas 4. Warm together the fat and 150g (6 oz) of the sugar in a large pan until the fat has melted. Cool slightly. Stir in the flour and eggs and beat well until smooth. Pour into a greased and lined 28 by 18cm (11 x 7 in) deep tin and bake for 35 minutes or until light golden in colour. Meanwhile mix together the lemon juice and the remaining sugar. When the cake is removed from the oven spoon the lemon mixture over the top. Cool in the tin until the lemon topping has sunk into the cake, then turn onto a cooling rack.

Chocolate Cake

> *90g (3½ oz) self raising flour*
> *15ml (1 tablespoon) cocoa*
> *100g (4 oz) soft brown sugar*
> *50g (2 oz) golden syrup*
> *75g (3 oz) margarine*
> *1 egg, beaten*
> *30ml (2 tablespoons) milk*

Preheat oven to 190°C (375°F)/Gas 5. Sift together the flour and cocoa. Warm together the sugar, syrup and fat until melted. Cool slightly. Add the warm mixture, egg and milk to the flour and beat well. Pour into a greased and lined 15cm (6 in) diameter deep cake tin. Bake for 40 minutes or until firm to the touch. Turn out and cool on a wire rack.

Boiled Fruit Cake

> *200ml (8 fl oz) milk*
> *100g (4 oz) margarine*
> *100g (4 oz) raisins*
> *150g (6 oz) currants*

150g (6 oz) sultanas
100g (4 oz) sugar
200g (8 oz) plain flour
5ml (1 teaspoon) bicarbonate of soda
pinch of salt
10ml (2 teaspoons) mixed spice
1 egg beaten

Preheat oven to 160°C (325°F)/Gas 3. Place the milk, fat, fruit and sugar in a pan, bring to the boil then simmer for 15 minutes. Cool slightly. Sift together the flour, soda, salt and spice. Beat in the cooled fruit mixture and the egg. Spoon into a greased and lined 17.5cm (7 in) diameter deep cake tin. Bake for 1½ hours or until a skewer pushed into the centre of the cake comes out cleanly.

Parkin

150g (6 oz) black treacle
50g (2 oz) golden syrup
75g (3 oz) soft brown sugar
75g (3 oz) margarine
200g (8 oz) self raising flour
10ml (2 teaspoons) ground ginger
10ml (2 teaspoons) mixed spices
100g (4 oz) fine or medium oatmeal
125ml (¼ pt) milk

Preheat oven to 160°C (325°F)/Gas 3. Melt treacle, syrup, sugar and margarine in a pan over a low heat. Stir until all the ingredients are blended. Do not allow the mixture to boil. Remove the pan from the heat and leave to cool. Sift flour and spices into a large bowl and stir in the oatmeal. Add the melted ingredients and milk to the dry ingredients and mix to a soft batter. Pour into a greased and lined 20cm (8 in) square cake tin and bake for one hour.

Oaty Raisin Bars

125g (5 oz) margarine
15ml (1 tablespoon) golden syrup
50g (2 oz) soft brown sugar
200g (8 oz) rolled oats
pinch of salt
50g (2 oz) seedless raisins

Preheat oven to 190°C (375°F)/Gas 5. Melt margarine, golden syrup and sugar in a pan over a low heat. Stir until all the ingredients are blended. Do not allow the mixture to boil. Remove pan from the heat and mix in the rolled oats, salt and raisins. Place mixture in a greased and lined 17.5cm (7 in) square cake tin and bake for 30 minutes or until golden brown in colour. Cool slightly then cut into fingers whilst still in tin. When cold, turn out.

German Apple Dessert Cake

> *100g (4 oz) butter or margarine*
> *100g (4 oz) caster sugar*
> *200g (8 oz) self raising flour*
> *pinch of salt*
> *2.5ml (½ teaspoon) cinnamon*
> *1 egg, beaten*
> *1 cooking apple sliced*
> *15ml (1 tablespoon) mincemeat*

Preheat oven to 180°C (350°F)/Gas 4. Melt the butter in a large pan over a low heat. Add the sugar, flour, salt, cinnamon and egg and beat well to form a smooth paste. Grease and line a 16cm (6½ in) round loose-bottomed cake tin. Place two thirds of mixture in tin and cover with sliced apple and mincemeat. Dot remaining cake mixture over apple. Bake for one hour until golden brown in colour. Leave to cool in tin for ten minutes before turning out.

Sponges

A true sponge is made of eggs, sugar and flour. It is deliciously light and should be eaten soon after baking as it does not keep. A fine soft flour is necessary as it has a lower gluten content. The whisking and folding in of the flour is the secret of the light open texture it needs. The proportion of eggs to flour and sugar is high, and if the eggs and sugar are whisked over heat the eggs thicken more easily. A balloon whisk will beat in more air than a rotary one, but the whole process is made much simpler if you have an electric mixer.

> *2 (size 4) standard eggs*
> *50g (2 oz) caster sugar*
> *50g (2 oz) plain flour*

This mixture is suitable for a 17.5cm (7 in) cake tin. Grease it well by brushing with vegetable oil. Have eggs at room temperature and see the flour is dry and not too cold. Preheat oven to 180°C (350°)/Gas 4.

If you are whisking by hand, put the eggs in a basin over hot water, but do not allow the hot water to touch the bottom of the basin. Whisk lightly then add sugar and continue whisking until the mixture is light and creamy. The mixture will become paler in colour and will 'leave a trail'. This means that a trail of the mixture will stay on the surface and not immediately blend in with what is underneath. Remove the basin from the pan of hot water and continue whisking until mixture is cool — about five minutes.

If you are using an electric whisk it is not necessary to have the bowl over hot water.

Sieve the flour over the surface and use a metal spoon to cut the flour into the froth. Use a slight flicking motion so that the flour is rolled in. The purpose is to lose as little air as possible when folding in the flour but to distribute it evenly. Transfer immediately to the cake tin, smooth the top and cook half way up the oven for about 20 minutes.

When cooked the cake should have shrunk slightly from the sides of the tin and if pressed gently with the finger no mark should be left. Cool the cake for a minute or two on a damp cloth as this will help you to remove the cake more easily. Invert it carefully onto a wire rack and lift the tin off carefully. If you don't want the cake to be marked by the wires use another rack to help you turn it right side up.

This basic sponge can be used on its own as a light cake to serve with compote of fruit. It can also be filled with any number of fruits combined with cream and served as a dessert. To make a sponge sandwich use a three egg mixture and bake in two 17.5cm (7 in) sandwich tins. When cool, spread generously with raspberry jam to layer the two cakes together, then dredge with caster sugar on top.

Swiss Roll
The recipe given will fill a swiss roll tin — a shallow baking tray measuring approx 25 by 15cm (6 in x 10 in). Line base of tray with greased, greaseproof paper. Bake above centre of oven for 7-8 minutes at 200°C (400°F)/Gas 6.

Turn out on to a piece of greaseproof paper dredged with caster or icing sugar and carefully invert the cake on to it. Spread with hot jam and roll up tightly.

If you plan to use jam and cream, roll up the cake whilst still hot with the sugared paper inside. When the cake has cooled unroll carefully, fill with jam and whipped cream and re-roll.

Chocolate Swiss Roll
Replace 15g (½ oz) of the flour with 15g (½ oz) cocoa and sieve with the flour.

When cool unroll and fill with Chocolate Butter Icing (see page 118)

Genoese
A genoese has a sponge like texture but it is firmer, richer and keeps longer. It is most often used for iced small cakes because it cuts well. Proportions are generally 25g (1 oz) caster sugar and 20g (¾ oz) butter, 20g (¾ oz) flour to each standard egg.

> *4 (size 4) standard eggs*
> *100g (4 oz) caster sugar*
> *75g butter or 45ml (3 tablespoons) vegetable oil*
> *75g (3 oz) plain flour*

Preheat oven to 180°C (350°F)/Gas 4. Make the genoese in the same way as a sponge cake until you have whisked the eggs and sugar over heat and continued whisking until cool. Melt the butter but put in a basin over hot water to prevent separating. Pour half butter or oil over mixture in a thin stream, then half the sieved flour. Pour over remaining butter or oil and sieved flour and cut in with a metal spoon to distribute flour and fat. Use as few movements as possible to avoid breaking down the volume.

Divide mixture equally between two greased and lined 20cm (8 in) sandwich tins and cook for 30 minutes or until mixture shrinks slightly from sides of tins.

Coffee Almond Cake

> *basic genoese sponge mixture, bake and allowed to cool*

For the butter icing:

> *100g (4 oz) butter*
> *200g (8 oz) icing sugar*
> *15ml (3 teaspoons) instant coffee powder*
> *30ml (2 tablespoons) milk (approx)*
> *50g (2 oz) almonds*

To assemble, beat the butter until soft and gradually add the sieved icing sugar mixed with coffee powder. Beat until blended, then gradually add enough milk to make an easy spreading consistency.

Toast the almonds under a grill until brown. Reserve half as halved almonds and chop the remainder finely. Take half the butter icing, mix in chopped almonds and use to sandwich the two layers of cake together. Spread remaining icing over the top and arrange the halved almonds in a pattern over the top.

Blackcurrant Gateau

> *basic genoese sponge mixture, baked and allowed to cool*
> *30ml (2 tablespoons) blackcurrant jam*
> *225g (8 oz) punnet blackcurrants*
> *glacé icing made with 375g (10 oz) icing sugar*
> *30ml (2 tablespoons) water*
> *1 tablespoon lemon juice*

For the frosting:

> *1 egg white*
> *50g (2 oz) caster sugar*

Sandwich the cakes together with blackcurrant jam mixed with half the fresh blackcurrants. Take remaining blackcurrants and divide into small sprigs. Paint each small sprig with egg white then dip or roll in the caster sugar. Carefully shake off any remaining sugar and allow to dry out on a wire rack.

Make the glacé icing. Sieve icing sugar into a bowl. Mix water with lemon juice and gradually beat in until icing will coat the back of a wooden spoon.

Cover the top and sides of the cake with the icing, using a round palette knife dipped in hot water to smooth the icing over evenly. Allow to set, then top with frosted blackcurrants.

Redcurrants can be used instead of blackcurrants, in which case use redcurrant jelly as the jam.

Loganberry Almond Cake

> *3 (grade 2) eggs*
> *75g (3 oz) plain flour*
> *25g (1 oz) ground almonds*
> *25g (1 oz) semolina*

1ml (¼ teaspoon) almond essence
1, 415g (14 oz) can loganberries
30ml (2 tablespoons) redcurrant jelly
125ml (¼ pt) cream

Whisk eggs and sugar until the mixture is thick, white and creamy and leaves a trail.

Sieve flour, ground almonds and semolina together and fold into the eggs mixture using a metal spoon. Stir in only enough to distribute the flour. Too much stirring at this stage will reduce the volume you have created during the whisking. Add almond essence.

Pour into a well greased 17.5cm (7 in) deep cake tin. Cook just above centre of oven at 180°C (350°F)/Gas 4 for about 35 minutes. Turn out and leave to cool on a wire rack.

Drain loganberries, retaining the juice. Prick the cake with a fork and pour juice over. Arrange loganberries on top. Melt redcurrant jelly in a saucepan and brush over the top of cake as a glaze.

Whip cream, then spread it around sides of cake. Chill until ready to serve.

Pineapple Gateau

3 egg sponge baked in 2 17.5cm (7 in) sandwich tins
411g (14½ oz) can pineapple pieces
30ml (2 tablespoons) rum (optional)
125ml (¼ pt) carton double cream

Make up the sponge as described in basic recipe and allow to cool. Drain can of pineapple pieces and retain juice. Pour juice carefully over the two sponges to moisten them. Put pineapple pieces in a basin and pour over the rum. Allow to stand for at least 30 minutes.

Whip cream, and use half the cream and half pineapple pieces, mixed, to layer the sponges together. Spread remaining whipped cream on top and arrange the other pineapple pieces in a pattern over.

Carrot Cake
A fatless sponge with an intriguing ingredient — grated carrot. Although carrot helps to keep it moist this cake does not keep for long.

100

100g (4 oz) grated carrot
3 large eggs
100g (4 oz) caster sugar
1 small lemon
50g (2 oz) semolina
50g (2 oz) ground almonds
50g (2 oz) plain flour
2.5ml (½ teaspoon) grated nutmeg

To decorate:

apricot jam, 30ml (2 tablespoons) whipped cream, sprinkling of caster sugar

Preheat oven to 170°C (325°F)/Gas 3. Grate carrot. Separate eggs. Place egg yolks and sugar together in a basin over hot water and whisk until thick and creamy. If using an electric whisk you can dispense with the hot water. Grate lemon rind and then add it with the juice to yolks. Whisk until blended. Stir in carrot, semolina, ground almonds and flour with nutmeg. Whisk egg whites until stiff then fold in. Grease and flour a 17.5cm (7 in) cake tin and pour in mixture. Bake in centre of oven for an hour. Leave to cool in tin a little while, then turn out on to a wire rack to cool.

Cut in half through the centre and sandwich together with apricot jam and whipped cream. Sprinkle with caster sugar before serving.

Quick Mix Cakes
Some cakes can be mixed quickly, either by putting all the ingredients in at one time or by the use of a vegetable oil as a fat. In these cases a higher proportion of baking powder is normally used to incorporate air into the cake and increase the volume. Sometimes the egg yolk and whites are separated so that the egg whites can be whisked until stiff before folding into the cake mixture and this increases the amount of air as well.

Orange Chocolate Cake

1 medium size orange
75ml (5 tablespoons) corn oil
125ml (5 oz) plain flour
10ml (2 teaspoons) baking powder
25g (1 oz) cocoa

125g (5 oz) caster sugar
2 (grade 3) eggs

Preset oven to 190°C (375°F)/Gas 5. Grate rind of orange. Cut in half and extract juice from half the orange. Set the other half to one side.

Put grated rind and juice into a measuring jug and make up to 80ml (3½ fl oz) with water. Sift flour, baking powder, cocoa and caster sugar into a bowl. Make a well in centre and pour in orange rind and juice, corn oil and the eggs. Mix as if mixing a batter, drawing in the flour gradually and beating until blended smoothly.

Oil a 17.5cm (7 in) deep cake tin and pour in batter. Bake in centre of oven for 25 minutes. Allow to cool in tin for a few minutes before turning out onto a wire rack. When cool cover top with glacé icing.

For the glacé icing:

100g (4 oz) icing sugar
juice from remaining half of orange

Sieve icing sugar into a bowl and gradually beat in orange juice then pour over top of cake allowing some to drip over the edges. Allow to set before serving.

Quick Mix Dundee Cake

100ml (4 fl oz) corn oil
150g (6 oz) caster sugar
3 (grade 4) eggs
450g (1 lb) mixed dried fruit
50g (2 oz) chopped almonds
50g (2 oz) glacé cherries
50g (2 oz) mixed peel
225g (8 oz) plain flour
10ml (2 teaspoons) baking powder
5ml (1 teaspoon) mixed spice
30ml (2 tablespoons) milk
50g (2 oz) split almonds

Preheat oven to 160°C (325°F)/Gas 3. Beat together oil, sugar and eggs. Add dried fruit, almonds, cherries and peel. Stir well together. Sieve flour with baking powder and spice and fold in to mixture with sufficient milk to form a soft dropping consistency.

Grease and line a 20cm (8 in) round deep cake tin. Transfer mixture to tin, smooth the top. Arrange split almonds on top.

Bake in centre of oven for 2-2¼ hours or until cake shrinks slightly from the sides of the tin. Allow to cool slightly before turning out onto a wire rack.

Honey Orange Loaf

> *100g (4 oz) soft margarine*
> *50g (2 oz) caster sugar*
> *2 medium oranges*
> *30ml (2 tablespoons) clear honey*
> *200g (8 oz) plain flour*
> *15ml (3 teaspoons) baking powder*
> *2 (grade 2) eggs*

Preheat oven to 180°C (350°F)/Gas 4. Grease a 900g (2 lb) loaf tin. Place all the ingredients except oranges into a mixing bowl. Grate rind from oranges and add 45ml (3 tablespoons) of the juice. Mix well with a wooden spoon or electric mixer until blended. Transfer to 900g (2 lb) loaf tin. Smooth top of mixture and bake in centre of oven for about 1¼ hours. Turn out and leave to cool on a wire rack.

Banana and Cherry Loaf

> *100g (4 oz) glacé cherries*
> *4 ripe bananas*
> *100g (4 oz) soft margarine*
> *150g (6 oz) soft brown sugar*
> *200g (8 oz) plain flour*
> *15ml (3 teaspoons) baking powder*
> *2 (grade 2) eggs*

Preheat oven to 160°C (325°F)/Gas 3. Grease a 900g (2 lb) loaf tin. Chop glacé cherries and mix in with the flour. Mash the bananas. Put all the ingredients into a bowl and beat together until well blended.

Transfer to the loaf tin. Smooth top of the mixture and bake in centre of oven for about 1¼ hours. Turn out and cool on a wire rack.

Glacé Fruit Loaf

> 150g (6 oz) soft margarine
> 150g (6 oz) caster sugar
> 3 (grade 4) eggs
> 100g (4 oz) sultanas
> 125g (5 oz) glacé cherries
> 25g (1 oz) chopped mixed peel
> 200g (8 oz) self raising flour
> 30ml (2 rounded tablespoons) apricot jam

Preheat oven to 160°C (325°F)/Gas 3. Put seven or eight of the glacé cherries aside. Chop the others and add to the flour. Put all the ingredients except the cherries you set aside and the jam into a mixing bowl and beat until blended. Transfer mixture to a well greased 900g (2 lb) loaf tin. Smooth the top and put the remaining cherries in a line down the middle. Bake in centre of oven for 1½ hours. Leave in tin for a few minutes before turning out onto a wire rack. Brush with the warmed apricot jam and leave until cool.

Honey Fudge Squares

> 100g (4 oz) plain flour
> 5ml (1 teaspoon) cinnamon
> 2.5ml (½ teaspoon) bicarbonate of soda
> pinch salt
> 45ml (3 tablespoons) vegetable oil
> 50g (2 oz) clear honey
> 50g (2 oz) black treacle
> 50g (2 oz) demerara sugar
> 1 (grade 2) egg with 30ml (2 tablespoons) milk

Preheat oven to 180°C (350°F)/Gas 4. Put all the ingredients into a mixing bowl and beat until well blended. Grease and line a 17.5cm (7 in) square cake tin and transfer the mixture. Bake for about 30 minutes or until firm. Cool on a wire rack. When cold cut into squares.

Quick Mix Scones

> 200g (8 oz) plain flour
> 2.5ml (½ teaspoon) salt
> 10ml (2 teaspoons) baking powder
> 30ml (2 tablespoons) corn oil
> 125ml (¼ pt) milk

Preheat oven to 220°C (425°F)/Gas 7. Grease a baking tray. Sieve flour, salt and baking powder into a bowl. Combine oil and milk and stir into flour until blended. Knead with your fingertips until dough is firm, smooth and elastic. Roll out to 6mm (¼ in) thick and cut into eight, 6cm (2½ in) rounds and put on the baking tray. Brush tops with milk and cook above centre of oven for about ten to twelve minutes. Cool on a wire rack.

Rich All in One Chocolate Cake
This is a very rich dark cake that keeps well — if it gets the chance.

> 175g (7 oz) plain flour
> 25g (1 oz) cocoa
> 2.5ml (½ teaspoon) salt
> 10ml (2 teaspoons) baking powder
> 5ml (1 teaspoon) bicarbonate of soda
> 5ml (1 teaspoon) powdered cinnamon
> 150g (6 oz) dark brown sugar
> 30ml (2 tablespoons) black treacle
> 2 (grade 4) eggs
> 150ml (6 fl oz) vegetable oil
> 150ml (6 fl oz) milk

For the cinnamon butter icing:

> 50g (2 oz) butter
> 150g (6 oz) icing sugar
> 10ml (2 teaspoons) powdered cinnamon
> 30ml (2 tablespoons) milk

To make the cake, preheat oven to 160°C (325°F)/Gas 3. Grease and line two, 20cm (8 in) sandwich tins.

Sift flour, cocoa, salt, baking powder, bicarbonate of soda and powdered cinnamon into a bowl. Add sugar. Make a well in the centre and add treacle, eggs, oil and milk. Stir in dry ingredients gradually, then beat together until blended. Pour the batter equally between the two sandwich tins. Bake just in centre of oven for 40-45 minutes. Leave to cool in tins for a few minutes then turn out onto a wire rack to cool. Sandwich together with cinnamon butter icing. The amounts given make enough icing to cover top and sandwich the two cakes.

Cinnamon butter icing: cream butter until really soft, then gradually add sifted icing sugar and cinnamon powder, beating well.

Add milk, beating all the time. Sandwich two cakes together then spread remainder on top and swirl with a fork to decorate.

Sponge Cake
You'll enjoy the texture of this sponge with the addition of vegetable oil.

> *125g (5 oz) plain flour*
> *25g (1 oz) cornflour*
> *10ml (2 teaspoons) baking powder*
> *2.5ml (½ teaspoon) salt*
> *125g (5 oz) caster sugar*
> *2 (grade 3) eggs*
> *90ml (3½ fl oz) corn oil*
> *90ml (3½ fl oz) water*
> *jam and caster sugar*

Preheat oven to 190°C (375°F)/Gas 5. Grease two 17.5cm (7 in) sandwich tins. Sieve flour, cornflour, baking powder, salt and sugar into a bowl. Separate eggs and mix the yolk with the oil and water then pour into the dry ingredients, beating steadily until a smooth batter is formed. Whisk egg whites stiffly and fold into the mixture. Divide into the two sandwich tins and bake just above centre of oven for 25-30 minutes. Leave for a few minutes before turning out on to a rack to cool. Spread with jam and sprinkle caster sugar on top.

Coffee Cake

> *125g (5 oz) plain flour*
> *10ml (2 teaspoons) baking powder*
> *pinch salt*
> *125g (5 oz) dark brown sugar*
> *75ml (5 tablespoons) vegetable oil*
> *30ml (2 tablespoons) milk*
> *15ml (1 tablespoon) instant coffee powder*
> *30ml (2 tablespoons) boiling water*
> *2 (grade 2) eggs*

Preheat oven to 190°C (375°F)/Gas 5. Well grease a 17.5cm deep cake tin. Sift flour, baking powder and salt into a bowl. Stir in the sifted sugar. Into a jug, put the oil and milk. Dissolve the coffee powder in the boiling water and add to jug. Separate white from yolks of eggs. Add egg yolks to oil etc. Make a well in the centre of the flour and pour in the contents of the jug, stirring the flour in slowly to

106

make a soft batter. Beat well until blended. Whisk egg whites stiffly and fold in to mix using a metal spoon. Work as lightly as possible so that the volume of air is not diminished. Transfer mixture to cake tin, smooth over the top and cook in centre of oven for about 30 minutes. Turn out and cool on a wire rack. Cover with butter icing.

For the coffee butter icing:

> 200g (8 oz) icing sugar
> 75g (3 oz) butter
> 5ml (1 teaspoon) instant coffee powder
> 30ml (2 tablespoons) boiling water

Beat butter with a wooden spoon until soft, then gradually beat in sifted icing sugar. Dissolve instant coffee in the boiling water, then gradually add to butter icing. When cake is cold cover top and sides with the icing.

Surprise Cream Cheese Cake
This is a 'proper' cake and not a dessert as its name could imply. As you can see, the surprise is the grated carrot which gives the cake an unusual and moist flavour and contrasts very pleasantly with the cream cheese topping.

> 150g (6 oz) grated carrot
> 150g (6 oz) caster sugar
> 2 (grade 2) eggs
> 75ml (3 fl oz) vegetable oil
> 200g (8 oz) plain flour
> 10ml (2 teaspoons) baking powder
> 2.5ml (½ teaspoon) salt
> 5ml (1 teaspoon) powdered cinnamon

For the topping:

> 100g (4 oz) cream cheese
> rind and juice of 1 small lemon
> 150g (6 oz) icing sugar

Grease a 17.5cm (7 in) deep cake tin. Preheat oven to 180°C (350°F)/Gas 4. Put all the ingredients for the cake into a bowl and stir until blended. Turn into a greased cake tin, smooth the top then bake below centre of oven for about an hour. Turn out and leave to cool on a wire rack.

To make the topping, mix the cream cheese with the rind and juice of the lemon. Beat in the sieved icing sugar. Put on top of the cake, swirl with a fork then leave it to set for an hour or two before serving.

Tea breads

Tea breads are a halfway house between cakes and bread and are extremely economical. Because they contain a small proportion of fat to flour and use fewer eggs with milk as a substitute, they do not keep as long. Try to eat them within a day or so of baking. You can spread butter on them if you wish, and this will certainly help if you feel they are getting dry. One thing is sure — they will be much enjoyed by a hungry family.

Treacle Tea Bread
This is a halfway house between cake and bread. It's lovely served in thick slices thinly spread with butter. Don't try to keep it — it's best eaten in two to three days.

> 150g (6 oz) wholemeal flour
> 150g (6 oz) plain flour
> 10ml (2 teaspoons) baking powder
> 75g (3 oz) butter
> 50g (2 oz) soft brown sugar
> 45ml (3 level tablespoons) black treacle
> 125ml (¼ pt) milk
> 1 (grade 2) egg

Preheat oven to 180°C (350°F)/Gas 4. Sift flour and baking powder into a bowl. Rub in butter until mixture resembles breadcrumbs. Stir in sugar. Mix treacle with milk and beat in egg. Pour into dry mixture. Beat with wooden spoon until well blended. If necessary add a little extra milk. Turn into a well greased 900g (2 lb) loaf tin. Spread the top smooth. Cook in centre of oven for 55-60 minutes. Leave to cool a little in the tin.

Country Herb Bread

200g (8 oz) wholemeal flour
5ml (1 teaspoon) salt
10ml (2 teaspoons) baking powder
25g (1 oz) butter or margarine
1 onion, finely chopped
2.5ml (½ teaspoon) dried mixed herbs
15ml (1 tablespoon) chopped parsley
125ml (¼ pt) milk

Preheat oven to 190°C (375°F)/Gas 5. Mix together the flour, salt and baking powder in a bowl. Rub in the fat. Add the onion, herbs and parsley. Stir in the milk and mix to a very soft dough. Place in a greased 450g (1 lb) small loaf tin, smooth the top and glaze with milk or beaten egg. Bake for 40-45 minutes.

Celery and Peanut Tea Bread

200g (8 oz) self raising flour
2.5ml (½ teaspoon) salt
pinch of pepper
25g (1 oz) butter or margarine
2 sticks celery, finely chopped
75g (3 oz) crunchy peanut butter
large pinch of garlic powder or 1 small clove garlic, finely chopped
1 egg, beaten
125ml (¼ pt) milk

Preheat oven to 190°C (375°F)/Gas 5. Sift together the flour, salt and pepper. Rub in the fat. Add the celery, peanut butter and garlic. Stir in the egg and milk and mix to a stiff dropping consistency. Spoon into a greased 450g (1 lb) small loaf tin. Smooth the top and glaze with milk if liked. Bake for 45-50 minutes.

Apple, Cheese and Walnut Loaf

200g (8 oz) self raising flour
2.5ml (½ teaspoon) salt
pinch of dry mustard
25g (1 oz) butter or margarine
1 medium sized cooking apple, peeled, cored and chopped

100g (4 oz) Lancashire cheese, grated
25g (1 oz) walnuts, chopped
1 egg, beaten
125ml (¼ pt) milk

Preheat oven to 190°C (375°F)/Gas 5. Sift together the flour, salt and mustard. Rub in the fat. Add the apple, cheese and walnuts. Stir in the egg and milk and mix to a dropping consistency. Spoon into a greased 450g (1 lb) small loaf tin. Bake for 50-60 minutes or until golden brown.

Festival Loaf
This is a kind of 'instant' birthday loaf. The mincemeat provides moisture and taste to an otherwise economical cake. The brandy adds extra flavour, but of course, you can use milk instead.

200g (8 oz) self raising flour
50g (2 oz) margarine
50g (2 oz) caster sugar
1 (grade 1) egg
half a standard 380g (14 oz) jar of mincemeat
30ml (2 tablespoons) brandy or milk

Preheat oven to 180°C (350°F)/Gas 4. Sieve flour into a bowl. Rub in margarine until mixture resembles fine breadcrumbs. Stir in sugar. Beat egg, then add with the mincemeat and brandy or milk, stirring until a soft dough is obtained. Well grease a 450g (1 lb) loaf tin, and pour in the mixture. Smooth the top. Bake in centre of oven for about one hour 15 minutes. Turn out and cool on a wire rack.

Cheese Loaf

200g (8 oz) plain flour
10ml (2 level teaspoons) baking powder
5ml (1 teaspoon) mustard powder
2.5ml (½ teaspoon) cayenne pepper
2.5ml (½ teaspoon) salt
75g (3 oz) butter
100g (4 oz) finely grated cheese
2 (grade 3) eggs
125ml (¼ pt) milk

Preheat oven to 180°C (350°F)/Gas 4. Sieve flour, baking powder,

111

mustard powder, cayenne pepper and salt into a bowl. Rub in butter until mixture resembles fine breadcrumbs. Stir in grated cheese. Beat eggs with milk and add to dry mixture to make a soft dropping consistency. Transfer to a well greased 450g (1 lb) loaf tin, smooth the top and bake in centre of oven for about 45 minutes. Turn out on a wire rack and leave to cool.

Pineapple Tea Cake

> 200g (8 oz) plain flour
> 2.5ml (½ level teaspoon) salt
> 10ml (2 level teaspoons) baking powder
> 50g (2 oz) butter
> 75g (3 oz) caster sugar
> 1, 450g (1 lb) can pineapple pieces
> 1 large (grade 1) egg

> For the glacé icing:

> 100g (4 oz) icing sugar
> 15ml (1 tablespoon) pineapple juice from can

Preheat oven to 190°C (375°F)/Gas 5. Sift flour, salt and baking powder into a bowl. Rub in butter until mixture resembles fine breadcrumbs. Stir in caster sugar. Drain pineapple, reserving the juice. Beat egg and stir in to mixture with the pineapple pieces. Mix with enough of the juice — about 30ml (2 tablespoons), to make a soft dough. Transfer to a 450g (1 lb) loaf tin, smooth the top and cook in the centre of the oven for about one hour. Turn out onto a wire rack and allow to cool.

To make the glacé icing, sieve icing sugar into a bowl and beat in 15ml (a tablespoon) of the pineapple juice until mixture is thick but runny. Spoon over the top of the cake and allow to set. When spooning the icing over the cake, place it on a wire rack with a plate underneath so that any spare glacé icing can be re-spooned over the top.

Prune and Walnut Tea Cake

> 100g (4 oz) plain wholemeal flour
> 200g (8 oz) plain flour
> 5ml (1 level teaspoon) baking powder
> 5ml (1 level teaspoon) baking soda

5ml (1 level teaspoon) salt
50g (2 oz) soft brown sugar
100g (4 oz) cooked prunes stoned and chopped coarsely
50g (2 oz) chopped walnuts
2 (grade 2) eggs
250ml (½ pt) plain yoghourt
30ml (2 tablespoons) vegetable oil

Preheat oven to 180°C (350°F)/Gas 4. Grease a 20cm (8 in) cake tin. Sift flours, baking powder, baking soda, salt together into a bowl. Add sugar and stir to blend well in. Add chopped prunes and most of the chopped walnuts, leaving a few to sprinkle on top. Beat eggs, mix with yoghourt and vegetable oil then pour into the flour mixture and stir until thoroughly blended. Transfer to a greased 20cm (8 in) cake tin and bake below centre of oven for one hour.

Spiced Ginger Tea Bread
An economical eggless recipe that can be eaten sliced on its own or spread with butter.

150g (6 oz) plain flour
2.5ml (½ teaspoon) salt
2.5ml (½ teaspoon) bicarbonate of soda
10ml (2 teaspoons) ground ginger
5ml (1 teaspoon) mixed spice
4 pieces stem ginger
50g (2 oz) lard
50g (2 oz) soft brown sugar
100g (4 oz) black treacle
15ml (1 tablespoon) syrup from stem ginger
30ml (2 tablespoons) milk

Preheat oven to 180°C (350°F)/Gas 4. Sift flour, salt, bicarbonate of soda, ground ginger and mixed spice into a bowl. Add chopped stem ginger. Over a very low heat melt lard, brown sugar and treacle. Stir briefly to mix ingredients then pour slowly into the flour and stir until blended. Add milk and ginger syrup. Pour into a lined 450g (1 lb) loaf tin. Set just below centre of oven and cook for 20 minutes. Reduce heat to 160°C (325°F)/Gas 3 and cook for another 35 minutes or until cooked. Remove from tin immediately and allow to cool on a wire rack. This cake should be kept wrapped or in a tin for 24 hours before cutting.

113

Peanut Loaf

To make two 450g (1 lb) loaves or one 900g (2 lb),

400g (1 lb) plain flour
15ml (3 teaspoons) baking powder
2.5ml (½ teaspoon) salt
100g (4 oz) lard
100g (4 oz) brown sugar
100g (4 oz) salted peanuts
1 large egg
250ml (½ pt) milk
45ml (3 flat tablespoons) crunchy peanut butter

Preheat oven to 180°C (350°F)/Gas 4. Sift flour, baking powder and salt into a bowl. Cut lard into small pieces and rub in until mixture resembles breadcrumbs. Sieve sugar or break down any lumps with the back of a spoon and stir into the flour. Chop the peanuts. Put the milk into a saucepan add the peanut butter and stir gently until butter has been absorbed into the milk. Leave it to cool a little. Stir half the chopped peanuts into the flour mixture, then make a well in the centre and add the beaten egg and the milk. Stir until blended. Put into two well greased 450g (1 lb) loaf tins or one 900g (2 lb) tin, smooth top flat, then press in the remaining chopped peanuts on top. Bake in the centre of the oven for one hour if using the smaller tins or for 1¼ hours for the larger one. Cool on a wire rack, then slice and serve with butter.

Christmas recipes

Christmas Pudding
To make one large and one small pudding

> *200g (8 oz) currants*
> *200g (8 oz) sultanas*
> *200g (8 oz) raisins*
> *50g (2 oz) mixed peel*
> *50g (2 oz) finely chopped almonds*
> *1 medium sized apple*
> *rind and juice of 1 lemon*
> *100g (4 oz) self raising flour*
> *5ml (1 teaspoon) mixed spice*
> *2.5ml (½ teaspoon) grated nutmeg*
> *150g (6 oz) shredded suet*
> *150g (6 oz) fresh breadcrumbs*
> *200g (8 oz) dark brown sugar*
> *3 (grade 4) eggs*
> *45ml (3 tablespoons) cold tea, ale or milk*

Check dried fruit, removing stalks etc. Chop mixed peel. Peel core and grate the apple. Grate rind from lemon, squeeze and retain the juice.

Sieve flour and spices into a large bowl. Mix in suet, breadcrumbs and sugar. Stir in dried fruit, peel, almonds, apple, lemon rind and juice. Beat eggs together in a bowl then add to the mixture with the tea, ale or milk. Don't despise the thought of using tea as it adds colour to the pudding.

Grease a 1 litre (2 pint) and ½ litre (1 pint) basin, then spoon in the mixture to fill about two thirds of each basin full. Smooth the top. Cover with a foil lid, then a cloth and boil for 6-8 hours in a pan of boiling water to give a rich dark colour. The water should come two thirds of the way up the basin and check from time to time to top up with more boiling water as necessary.

When cooked, remove wet paper and cloths, rewrap in fresh greaseproof paper and keep in a cool dry and airy cupboard. On Christmas Day boil again for 2-3 hours.

Christmas Cake

Because of the long cooking time involved, I've known more correspondence about burned Christmas cakes than practically anything else. The time can only be a guide here, because ovens are individual things and can vary. Keep an eye on your cake after the first three hours or less if you are making a smaller version. Test by inserting a skewer in the middle of the cake. It should come out cleanly and the mixture will have shrunk slightly from the sides of the tin. If it looks as if it is getting too brown during the cooking, put a piece of brown paper over the top of it.

225g (8 oz) butter
225g (8 oz) soft brown sugar
225g (8 oz) plain flour
2.5ml (½ teaspoon) salt
2.5ml (½ teaspoon) mixed spice
2.5ml (½ teaspoon) grated nutmeg
5ml (1 teaspoon) cocoa
50g (2 oz) glacé cherries
4 (grade 2) eggs
15ml (1 tablespoon) black treacle
225g (8 oz) EACH of currants, raisins, sultanas
50g (2 oz) candied peel
50g (2 oz) chopped almonds
45-60ml (3-4 tablespoons) brandy or sherry (optional)

Line the sides and base of a 20cm (8 in) deep cake tin and put a piece of brown paper that extends 5cm (2 in) above the edge around the outside to protect the cake whilst cooking.

Set the oven to 150°C (300°F)/Gas 2. Cream butter and sugar together until soft and creamy in texture. Sift flour, salt, spices and cocoa together. Check dried fruit, removing any stalks. Chop glacé cherries roughly and dust them lightly in the flour. Beat eggs and add a little at a time to butter mixture with 15ml (a tablespoon) of flour to prevent curdling. Add black treacle, stirring well. Fold in remaining flour, then add dried fruit, cherries, peel and chopped almonds. Mix together then spoon into the tin. Smooth the top. Bake in centre of the oven for 3½ to 4 hours, but read note at top and test after 3 hours and at regular intervals after. A few days before covering with almond icing, prick the top of the cake with a thin skewer and carefully spoon over the alcohol.

White Fruit Cake

This is a lovely cake for a celebration when you don't want it too rich. The glacé cherries and peel add a festive air and the ground almonds keep the cake moist.

> *225g (8 oz) butter*
> *225g (8 oz) caster sugar*
> *100g (4 oz) glacé cherries*
> *225g (8 oz) plain flour*
> *3 (grade 2) eggs*
> *100g (4 oz) mixed peel*
> *50g (2 oz) ground almonds*
> *few drops almond essence*

> For the glacé icing:

> *225g (8 oz) icing sugar*
> *45ml (3 tablespoons) lemon juice*
> *extra cherries for decoration with angelica*

Preheat oven to 150°C (300°F)/Gas 2. Cream butter and sugar together until light and creamy and the sugar has lost its gritty taste. Cut glacé cherries in half and dust them lightly in the flour. Break eggs into creamed mixture one at a time adding a little flour with each addition to prevent curdling. Add remaining flour with the cherries and mixed peel, then stir in the ground almonds with three or four drops of almond essence.

Transfer to a greased and lined 17.5cm (7 in) deep cake tin and bake just below centre of oven for about two hours.

Turn on to a wire rack to cool.

To decorate, sieve icing sugar into a bowl and gradually beat in the lemon juice. Cover cake with two or three coats, and arrange a flower motif on top using the halved glacé cherries and the angelica as stalks.

Mince Pies

100g (4 oz) shortcrust or rough puff pastry (see pages 3 and 31)
100g (4 oz) mincemeat
milk and caster sugar for glaze

Roll out pastry thinly. Grease patty tins and cut a circle slightly larger than the tins. Keep the best circles for the tops. Put a circle of pastry into each tin, add 5ml (a heaped teaspoon) of mincemeat. Dampen edges and cover with remaining pastry circles. Press the edges together well. Brush with milk and sprinkle a little caster sugar on top.
Bake as for the pastry you have chosen.

Chocolate Log Cake

50g (2 oz) butter
100g (4 oz) caster sugar
2 (grade 2) eggs
2.5ml (½ teaspoon) vanilla essence
75g (3 oz) self raising flour
25g (1 oz) cocoa

For the chocolate butter icing:

75g (3 oz) plain chocolate
100g (4 oz) butter
150g (6 oz) icing sugar
Imitation robin and holly to decorate
sprinkling of white icing sugar

Preheat oven to 200°C (400°F)/Gas 6. Grease and line a swiss roll tin, 28.5 by 17.5cm (11 x 7 in). Beat butter to soften, add caster sugar and beat until soft and creamy. Add eggs, vanilla essence, gradually. Sift flour with cocoa and fold gently into the mix with a metal spoon.

Transfer to the tin, smooth the top, then bake for ten minutes. Have ready an extra sheet of greaseproof paper and sprinkle with sugar. Trim the edges of the cake with a sharp knife. Roll up the cake with the greaseproof paper inside, and leave to cool. Unroll carefully when cool, remove paper and spread with the icing.

To make the icing, melt the chocolate in a basin over warm water. Cream the butter and add the icing sugar slowly, then gradually add the melted chocolate. Use one third of the icing to spread the opened

118

out cake. Re roll. Spread the remaining icing all over the cake so that it is completely covered. Mark into ridges with a fork, lengthwise over the sides of the cake and in a circular motion over either end. Put the robin and holly leaves on top and sprinkle with a little extra icing sugar to give a snow effect.

Cooking with yeast

Once mastered, bread-making can be a satisfying skill, enhanced by knowing that you are working with a small living organism, yeast, which grows as it starts to work in the dough.

Bread was initially unleavened and wafer-thin. Baking started being looked upon as a skilled craft by the Egyptians who introduced different varieties of breads. Later, baking became an important profession. Nowadays, once we understand the workings of the different ingredients and processes, there are endless varieties of sweet and savoury doughs to be tried.

Firstly, let us take a look at the main ingredients used in bread-making and answer some of the questions that will give a better understanding of the whole process.

Yeast

Yeast is a living organism which needs warmth and moisture to enable it to grow. It can be obtained as fresh compressed yeast which can sometimes be purchased from bakers who make their own bread on the premises, or from some health food stores; or dried yeast which is sold as granules in packets and tins, and is more readily available. Dried yeast is less perishable than fresh, which should be stored in the refrigerator, where it will keep for about four weeks if wrapped in a plastic bag. You can tell if it is still fresh as it should be creamy in colour and not too crumbly. Tins of dried yeast will keep for about six months in a cool place; the packets do not keep as long.

The proportion of yeast to flour will depend upon the type of bread. More is required for a wholemeal bread than for a plain white bread, as this gives a heavier dough. More is also required for enriched doughs with extra ingredients such as eggs and fruit and more sugar.

For a plain dough, fresh yeast can be rubbed into the flour or mixed into the liquid. For a richer dough, yeast is mixed with a proportion of the flour, all the liquid and a little sugar to form a batter, then left in a warm place until frothy. It is then mixed with the other ingredients in the recipe.

Fresh yeast requires a warm liquid to activate it, and can then be used straight away, whereas dried yeast requires a hand-hot liquid, and has then to be left in the liquid about ten minutes to dissolve and become frothy.

Yeast needs warmth and moisture to give off the bubbles of gas which causes the dough to rise.

Flour

Flour plays a considerable part in helping the bread to rise. It contains a protein substance called gluten. When the flour is mixed with the liquid and kneaded, the gluten stretches, forming an elastic network which holds the air bubbles given off by the yeast as it starts to grow, giving a loaf of a good volume. It is therefore important to knead the dough well, as this strengthens the gluten and makes it more elastic.

Plain flour and a 'strong' or bread flour is best for bread-making as this is sturdier and contains more gluten. Wholemeal flour has less gluten than white flour, so wholemeal breads are usually heavier and have less volume than plain white bread. Other flours and grains such as rye, cracked wheat, bran and wheatgerm, can be added to give more variety. These often need to be combined with a strong white flour, as they lack sufficient gluten in themselves to provide a good bread structure.

Flour supplies carbohydrate, protein, vitamins and minerals to our daily diet. As a general rule, wholemeal flour contains a little more protein, vitamins, particularly of the B group, and minerals than white flour. Bran in wholemeal flour gives roughage.

Liquids

Liquids used in the doughs are mainly milk and water. Milk gives a softer crust and improves the texture; water gives a crisper crust.

Other ingredients used in bread-making

Sugar: this stimulates the growth of yeast. White sugar is usually used, but brown sugar, molasses or honey can be used instead.

Fat: butter, margarine, lard or cooking oil are used for flavour, improving the texture and the keeping quality of the breads.

Salt: this adds flavour and controls the growth of the yeast. Too much could take the dough longer to rise.

Eggs: improve the colour, flavour, texture and food value.

Fruit and nuts: add flavour and variety, but do make the rising time take longer.

Stages in bread-making
The best way to add the liquid to the flour is to add it all at once. Mix it into the flour and do not press the dough together until you can tell that the dough will be soft enough. It is better to have a dough which is too sticky as it is easier to add flour to this than to add liquid to a stiff dough. As the absorption properties of the flours varies, it is important to gain experience in knowing when the dough feels right and when there is enough liquid.

Kneading is very necessary as it strengthens the gluten which helps to give a good textured and volumed bread.

To knead the dough
If the dough is at all sticky, place on a lightly floured surface (if the dough is of the right consistency, then extra flour should not be required). Stretch dough and fold towards you with one hand, supporting it with the other, then push away with the palms of the hands. Turn the dough one quarter round and continue stretching, folding and turning, making a rhythmic motion. If you are hand-mixing the dough, knead for about ten minutes, or until it feels smooth, elastic and no longer sticky, adding more flour if necessary. Kneading will not take so long if you are using a mixer with a dough hook.

To test whether dough has been sufficiently kneaded make an indentation in the dough with your finger, and the dough should spring back.

A warm, moist atmosphere is necessary for the yeast to work when the dough is rising. (If your kitchen is not warm enough, the bowl containing the dough can be placed on a rack above a larger bowl of hot water, and the steam will provide the necessary conditions.) Place the dough in a lightly greased bowl and cover with plastic cling wrap or foil to prevent a crust from forming. Rising will not occur if the conditions are too cold, or if too much fat, salt and sugar are used. Also, if the liquid in which the yeast was dissolved was too hot, then this will kill the yeast. Allow the dough to rise until it has doubled in size. The dough should then feel soft and puffy. The

122

term 'knocking back' the dough refers to when it is re-kneaded after the initial rising, and punched with your fist to remove any air bubbles. The dough is then ready for shaping. For a description of different ways to shape breads, turn to page 127.

The bread can be glazed according to the required finish. Beaten egg can be used, water, butter, or a combination of milk or water and sugar. Plain bread loaves are made more attractive when sprinkled with sesame or poppy seeds, cracked wheat, oats, crushed cornflakes, or any variety of seeds and grains.

Bread requires a hot oven to kill the yeast and set the gluten. The bread should not rise after it goes into the oven, and should therefore be completely risen before baking. For a plain white or wholemeal bread, pre-heat the oven to 230°C (450°F)/Gas 8, for enriched breads preheat to 190-220°C (375-425°F)/Gas 5-7.

To test whether bread is cooked tap underneath with your knuckles. If the bread sounds hollow, it is done. Once baked, the bread should be left to cool on a cooling rack, and not stored or wrapped until quite cold, or it will soften the bread and make it doughy. Store packed in polythene bags, tied securely, in a cool place, or freeze. Baked bread freezes very well when packed in airtight plastic freezer bags or wrapped in foil. Freeze whilst the bread is very fresh, label and date the packages. The plain baked doughs will keep in the freezer for about six months, and the enriched doughs for four months. When ready to use, thaw at room temperature from between three to six hours depending on the size of the bread, or about 1½ hours for rolls. Alternatively, if you are in a hurry, thaw bread in the oven. Wrap frozen bread in foil and place loaves in a moderate oven for about ¾ hour, or rolls in a very hot oven for 10-15 minutes. Unbaked dough can also be frozen successfully. If you are going to do this, increase the quanitity of yeast used in the recipe by half as much again, and place the unrisen dough into greased freezer bags, leaving space for rising. Freeze immediately and store for up to eight weeks. An enriched dough will store for up to five weeks. When ready to use, the bag should be opened and re-sealed to allow room for rising, and left at room temperature for three to four hours, or in the refrigerator overnight. When doubled in size the dough is then ready to be 'knocked back' and shaped.

Short time bread-making method
This is a quick method which has an additional ingredient, ascorbic acid or vitamin C. Ascorbic acid strengthens the gluten in the flour,

and also extra yeast is used to speed up the rising. This is because with this method the initial rising process required for traditional breads is missed out, and replaced by a five to ten minute rest period, which makes it a much quicker method. With the short-time doughs better results are achieved if fresh rather than dried yeast is used, as the dried tends to give rather a yeasty flavour to the bread.

Some problems that may occur in bread-making
Q   What causes a dough not to rise?
A   Probably the yeast may be stale and therefore inactive, or the dough may have been too stiff and heavy. Always make sure sufficient liquid is added to the dough in the initial mixing.
Q   What can be done if you find you have started to make the dough, but run out of time to complete the process?
A   Allow the dough to rise once, knock it back, place in refrigerator and cover with greased polythene or plastic cling wrap. Then, when you are ready to use it the next day, simply remove it from the refrigerator and allow the dough to rise in a warm place until doubled in size. Then shape, rise and bake in the usual manner.
Q   What can be done if the bread has over-risen before being baked?
A   If this has happened, simply turn it out, knead it lightly and re-shape it. Leave it to rise again until double in size, and bake.
Q   Why does the dough sometimes spill out over the tin during baking?
A   This could be because the mixture has been put into too small a tin, or the salt, which checks the growth of the yeast, was missed out causing the dough to rise too much, or the oven temperature was wrong.
Q   Why is it that air-holes sometimes appear in the middle of baked loaves?
A   This is because the air has not been knocked out before the dough was shaped. 'Knocking-back' the dough is an important process.

Basic White Bread
Makes one large or two small loaves

15g (½ oz) fresh yeast or 10ml (2 level teaspoons) dried yeast
450ml (¾ pt) warm water
675g (1½ lb) strong plain white flour
15ml (1 level tablespoon) salt
15g (½ oz) margarine
beaten egg or milk to glaze

Crumble fresh yeast into warm water and stir to dissolve. (If using dried yeast, dissolve one level teaspoon (1 x 5ml) caster sugar in 450ml (¾ pt) hand-hot water. Sprinkle dried yeast on top and leave about ten minutes until frothy.) Mix flour and salt in a bowl and rub in margarine. Mix yeast liquid into flour. Turn out dough and sprinkle surface lightly with flour if dough is at all sticky. Knead dough, stretching and folding, until it feels firm and elastic and no longer sticky. Place dough in a lightly greased bowl, cover with greased polythene, foil or plastic cling wrap, and leave to rise in a warm place until doubled in size. 'Knock-back' the dough by re-kneading and punching out any air bubbles, until dough feels smooth. Weigh off 450g (1 lb) of risen dough for a 450g (1 lb) loaf tin or 900g (2 lb) of risen dough for a 900g (2 lb) loaf tin. Flatten the dough to the width and length of the tin, press into greased tin. (Alternatively, use the basic white bread recipe for any of the other shapes given on page 127.) Use any remaining dough for rolls. Cover loaves or rolls with greased polythene or plastic cling wrap, and leave to rise in a warm place until doubled in size or risen to the top of the loaf tin. Preheat oven to 230°C (450°F)/Gas 8. Brush dough with beaten egg or milk to glaze if wished, and sprinkle with poppy or sesame seeds if wished. Bake in centre of oven for 30 to 40 minutes if in a tin, 25 to 35 minutes if loaf is cooked on a baking sheet. For cooking instructions for rolls see page 128. To test if cooked, tap bread underneath; it should sound hollow. Place on a wire rack to cool.

Basic Brown Bread
Makes one large or two small loaves

> *25g (1 oz) fresh yeast or 15ml (1 level tablespoon) dried yeast*
> *450ml (¾ pt) warm water*
> *675g (1½ lb) wheatmeal flour*
> *15ml (1 level tablespoon) salt*
> *15g (½ oz) margarine*
> *beaten egg or milk to glaze*

Crumble fresh yeast into warm water and stir to dissolve. (If using dried yeast, dissolve one level teaspoon (1 x 5ml) caster sugar in 450ml (¾ pt) hand-hot water. Sprinkle dried yeast on top and leave about ten minutes until frothy.) Mix flour and salt in a bowl and rub in margarine. Mix yeast liquid into flour. Turn out dough and sprinkle surface lightly with flour if dough is at all sticky. Knead dough, stretching and folding, until it feels firm and elastic and no

125

longer sticky. Place dough in a lightly greased bowl, cover with greased polythene, foil or plastic cling wrap, and leave to rise in a warm place until doubled in size. 'Knock-back' the dough by re-kneading and punching out any air bubbles, until dough feels smooth. Weigh off 450g (1 lb) of risen dough for a 450g (1 lb) loaf tin or 900g (2 lb) of risen dough for a 900g (2 lb) loaf tin. Flatten the dough to the width and length of the tin, press into greased tin. (Alternatively, use the basic brown bread recipe for any of the other shapes given on page 127.) Use any remaining dough for rolls. Cover loaves or rolls with greased polythene or plastic cling wrap, and leave to rise in a warm place until doubled in size, or risen to the top of the loaf tin. Preheat oven to 230°C (450°F)/Gas 8. Brush dough with beaten egg or milk to glaze if wished, and sprinkle with seeds or grains if wished, e.g. poppy seeds, cracked wheat. Bake in centre of oven for 30 to 40 minutes if in a tin, 25 to 35 minutes if loaf is cooked on a baking sheet. For cooking instructions for rolls see page 128. To test if cooked, tap bread underneath; it should sound hollow. Place on a wire rack to cool.

Short-time White Bread
Makes one large or two small loaves

> *25g (1 oz) fresh yeast*
> *425ml (14 fl oz) warm water*
> *25mg ascorbic acid tablet*
> *675g (1½ lb) strong plain white flour*
> *10ml (2 level teaspoons) salt*
> *5ml (1 level teaspoon) caster sugar*
> *15g (½ oz) margarine*
> *beaten egg or milk to glaze*

Crumble fresh yeast into warm water, crush ascorbic acid tablet and stir into yeast to dissolve. Mix flour, salt and sugar in a bowl and rub in margarine. Mix yeast liquid into flour. Turn out dough and sprinkle surface lightly with flour if dough is at all sticky. Knead dough, stretching and folding until it feels firm and elastic and no longer sticky, for ten minutes. (It is important for the short-time dough to be kneaded very well at this stage, to make the dough more elastic.) Place dough in a greased polythene bag and leave to rest for five to ten minutes. Turn out dough; 'knock-back' the dough by re-kneading and punching out any air bubbles, until dough feels smooth. Weigh off 450g (1 lb) of dough for a 450g (1 lb) loaf tin or 900g (2 lb) dough for a 900g (2 lb) loaf tin. Flatten the dough to the width and length of the tin, press into greased tin. (Alternatively use this basic recipe for any of the other shapes given below.) Use any remaining dough for rolls. Cover loaves or rolls with greased polythene or plastic cling wrap, and leave to rise in a warm place until doubled in size, or risen to the top of the loaf tin. Preheat oven to 230°C (450°F)/Gas 8. Brush dough with beaten egg or milk to glaze if wished, and sprinkle with poppy or sesame seeds if wished. Bake in centre of oven for 30 to 40 minutes if in a tin, 25 to 35 minutes if loaf is cooked on a baking sheet. To test if cooked, tap bread underneath; it should sound hollow. Place on a wire rack to cool.

Shaping bread dough
Loaves
Cottage loaf. Weigh off 450g (1 lb) of risen dough. Cut off one quarter of this and knead and shape the two pieces of dough into round balls. Place the smaller ball of dough on top of the larger, and with a floured finger press through the centre of the small one through to the large one. Place on a greased baking sheet.

Coburg loaf. Weigh off 450g (1 lb) of risen dough. Knead and shape into a ball. Place on a greased baking sheet and make a cross on top of dough with a sharp knife.

Cob loaf. Weigh off 450g (1 lb) of risen dough. Knead and shape into a ball. Place on a greased baking sheet. Flatten slightly.

Flowerpot loaf. Grease an earthenware flowerpot. Knead dough, amount will depend on size of flowerpot; but dough should approximately half fill the container. Press dough into flowerpot. (If you are using a new flowerpot, grease well and leave in a fairly hot oven for about 30 minutes before using, to draw out any moisture which could cause the bread to stick. Do not wet the flowerpot, simply wipe out after use.)

Tin loaf. Weigh off 450g (1 lb) of risen dough for a 450g (1 lb) loaf tin and 900g (2 lb) of risen dough for a 900g (2 lb) loaf tin. Flatten the dough to the width and length of the tin; press into greased tin.

Plait loaf. Weigh off 450g (1 lb) or 900g (2 lb) of risen dough (depending on size of loaf required). Divide dough into three and roll each piece with the hands to form a long roll. Gather together one end of each roll and press firmly together. Plait half way down, then turn over and complete plaiting. Seal ends and tuck underneath. Place on a greased baking sheet.

Cake Tin Loaves. Press dough into a greased round deep cake tin.

Amount will depend on the size of tin; dough should approximately half fill the container.

Baking.

Cover loaves with greased polythene or plastic cling wrap, and leave to rise in a warm place until doubled in size, or risen to the top of the loaf tin. Preheat oven to 230°C (450°F)/Gas 8. Brush dough with beaten egg or milk to glaze if wished, and sprinkle with seeds or grains, e.g. poppy seeds, cracked wheat. Bake in centre of oven 30 to 40 minutes if in a tin, 25 to 35 minutes if on a baking sheet, depending on size of loaf. To test if cooked, tap bread underneath; it should sound hollow. Place on a wire rack to cool.

Rolls

Weigh off 50g (2 oz) to 75g (3 oz) risen dough for each roll, and shape in any of the following ways.

Knot. Roll piece of dough with the hands into a long thin roll. Tie loosely into a knot.

Cloverleaf. Divide piece of dough into three. Shape each piece into a ball and place close together in the shape of a cloverleaf.

Coil. Roll piece of dough with the hands into a long thin roll. Curl dough, starting from outside, working into centre to form a coil.

Twist. Divide piece of dough into two. Roll each piece with the hands to form a long thin roll. Press ends together, twist dough together and seal ends, tucking them underneath.

Plain rolls. Shape each piece of dough into a ball with the fingers. Work into a round shape, making a circular movement with the palm of the hand arched over the dough.

Baking.

Place rolls well apart on a greased baking sheet. Cover with greased polythene or plastic cling wrap and leave to rise in a warm place until doubled in size. Preheat oven to 230°C (450°F)/Gas 8. Brush rolls with beaten egg or milk, if wished, and sprinkle with seeds or grains, e.g. poppy seeds, cracked wheat. Bake on second from top shelf of oven for 15 to 20 minutes, until golden brown. To test if cooked, tap rolls underneath; they should sound hollow.

Basic Enriched Dough

Batter mix:

> *200ml (8 fl oz) warm milk*
> *15g (½ oz) fresh yeast or 10ml (2 level teaspoons) dried yeast*
> *125g (5 oz) strong plain white flour*
> *5ml (1 level teaspoon) caster sugar*

Dough:

275g (11 oz) strong plain white flour
5ml (1 level teaspoon) salt
50g (2 oz) margarine
1 egg

Blend milk and yeast together in a large bowl. Mix in remaining batter ingredients, cover and leave in a warm place about 20 minutes, or until frothy. Mix flour and salt in a bowl and rub in margarine. Beat egg and add to batter mix with the flour. Mix to form a soft dough. Turn out dough and sprinkle surface lightly with flour if dough is at all sticky. Knead dough, stretching and folding until it feels firm and elastic and no longer sticky. Place dough in a lightly greased bowl, cover with greased polythene, foil or plastic cling wrap, and leave to rise in a warm place until doubled in size. 'Knock-back' the dough by re-kneading and punching out any air bubbles, until dough feels smooth.

Use this basic recipe for any of the following recipes.

Cornish Splits
Makes 12

one quantity risen enriched dough (see basic recipe page 128)
whipped double cream or clotted cream
raspberry or strawberry jam
icing sugar to dredge

Divide dough into twelve pieces. Form each piece into a ball with the fingers and place well apart on greased baking sheets. (Keep unworked pieces of dough covered while shaping buns, to prevent drying out.) Cover with greased polythene or plastic cling wrap, and leave to rise in a warm place until doubled in size. Preheat oven to 220°C (425°F)/Gas 7. Bake buns on second from top shelf of oven for 15 to 20 minutes until golden brown. To test if cooked, tap buns underneath; they should sound hollow. Place on a wire rack to cool. Make a diagonal cut from top to centre of each bun. Fill with cream and jam and dredge with icing sugar.

Chelsea Buns
Makes 9

½ quantity enriched dough (see basic recipe page 128)

For the filling:

15g (½ oz) butter
75g (3 oz) mixed dried fruit
25g (1 oz) demerara sugar
grated rind one lemon
5ml (1 rounded teaspoon) mixed spice

For the glaze:

15ml (1 level tablespoon) caster sugar
30ml (2 tablespoons) hot water

Roll dough to an oblong about 30cm by 20cm (12 x 8 in). Melt the butter and brush over dough. Sprinkle remaining filling ingredients over the top to within 1.25cm (½ in) of the edges. Roll up from the long side like a swiss roll and seal edges. Cut into nine equal pieces and place flat in lines of three, close to each other but not quite touching, in a greased 17.5cm (7 in) square cake tin. Cover with greased polythene or plastic cling wrap, and leave to rise in a warm place until doubled in size. Preheat oven to 200°C (400°F)/Gas 6. Bake in centre of oven for 25 to 30 minutes until golden brown. Remove from oven. Mix sugar and water together and brush over buns whilst still warm.

Pizza Rolls

1 small onion
1 clove garlic
75g (3 oz) Mozarella cheese
50g (2 oz) pepperoni (or 4 rashers streaky bacon, grilled)
15ml (1 tablespoon) oil
5ml (1 level teaspoon) dried oregano
salt and pepper
½ quantity enriched dough (see basic recipe page 128)
15ml (1 level tablespoon) tomato purée
beaten egg or milk to glaze
sesame seeds, optional

Peel and chop onion; crush garlic; grate cheese and finely chop pepperoni (or crumble bacon if used). Heat oil and fry onion and garlic until soft. Stir in oregano, salt and pepper. Roll dough to an oblong 30cm by 22.5cm, (12 x 9 in). Spread tomato purée over the dough. Sprinkle over onion mixture, cheese and pepperoni. Roll up from the long side and place on a greased baking sheet with the join underneath. Cover with greased polythene or plastic cling wrap, and leave to rise in a warm place until doubled in size. Preheat oven to 200°C (400°F)/Gas 6. Make diagonal cuts across the top of the dough (be careful not to go through to the filling). Brush top with beaten egg or milk to glaze, and sprinkle with sesame seeds if wished. Bake in centre of the oven for 20 to 25 minutes until golden brown. To test if cooked, tap loaf underneath; it should sound hollow. This is best served warm.

Stollen

> 25g (1 oz) glacé cherries
> 25g (1 oz) almonds
> 25g (1 oz) raisins
> 50g (2 oz) sultanas
> grated rind one lemon
> ½ quantity enriched dough (see basic recipe page 128)
> 15g (½ oz) butter
> icing sugar to dredge

Finely chop glacé cherries and almonds; mix with raisins, sultanas and lemon rind. Place dough on a lightly floured surface, flatten slightly and sprinkle on fruit mixture. Carefully knead fruit into dough until well mixed, adding more flour if necessary. Roll dough to an oval 20cm by 25cm (8 x 10 in). Melt butter and brush a little over dough. Fold dough in two lengthwise, almost to the middle. Form into a crescent shape and place on a greased baking sheet. Cover with greased polythene or plastic cling wrap, and leave to rise in a warm place until doubled in size. Preheat oven to 200°C (400°F)/ Gas 6. Brush top of stollen with remaining melted butter and bake in centre of oven for 25 to 30 minutes until golden brown. To test if cooked, tap stollen underneath; it should sound hollow. Place on a wire rack to cool, dredge top with icing sugar.

Continental Fruit Crescent

> 1 eating apple
> 1 pear
> 25g (1 oz) almonds
> 25g (1 oz) butter
> 50g (2 oz) soft brown sugar

25g (1 oz) raisins
grated rind of one orange
½ quantity enriched dough (see basic recipe page 128)

For the icing:

50g (2 oz) icing sugar
10-15ml (2 to 3 teaspoons) fresh orange juice
few chopped almonds

Peel, core and slice apple and pear. Chop almonds. Melt butter in a small pan and cook fruit until soft, but not broken. Remove from heat, stir in sugar, almonds, raisins and orange rind. Drain off any excess juice from fruit and reserve. Leave fruit to cool. Roll dough to an oblong about 30cm by 22.5cm (12 x 9 in). Brush a little of the reserved juice over the dough. Spread filling over the top to within 1.25cm (½ in) of the edges. Roll up from the long side and place on a greased baking sheet with the join underneath. Form into a crescent shape, and make 2.5cm (1 in) cuts just through to the filling. Cover with greased polythene or plastic cling wrap, and leave to rise in a warm place until doubled in size. Preheat oven to 200°C (400°F)/ Gas 6. Bake in centre of the oven for 20 to 25 minutes. Brush top of the crescent with any remaining fruit juices and return to the oven for a further minute. Place on a wire rack to cool. Sieve icing sugar and blend with orange juice until smooth and coats the back of a spoon. Trickle icing over the crescent and sprinkle with a few chopped almonds.

Sticky Fruit Tea Buns
Makes 10

For the batter mix:

200ml (8 fl oz) warm milk
15g (½ oz) fresh yeast or 10ml (2 level teaspoons) dried yeast
125g (5 oz) strong plain white flour
5ml (1 level teaspoon) caster sugar

For the dough:

275g (11 oz) strong plain white flour
5ml (1 level teaspoon) salt
50g (2 oz) margarine
50g (2 oz) caster sugar

25g (1 oz) currants
50g (2 oz) sultanas
25g (1 oz) cut mixed peel
1 egg

For the glaze:

15ml (1 tablespoon) caster sugar
15ml (1 tablespoon) milk

Blend milk and yeast together in a large bowl. Mix in remaining batter ingredients, cover and leave in a warm place about 20 minutes or until frothy. Mix flour and salt in a bowl and rub in margarine. Stir in sugar, fruit and peel. Beat egg and add to batter mix with the flour. Mix to form a soft dough. Turn out dough and sprinkle surface lightly with flour if dough is at all sticky. Knead dough, stretching and folding until it feels firm and elastic and no longer sticky. Place dough in a lightly greased bowl, cover with greased polythene, foil or plastic cling wrap, and leave to rise in a warm place until doubled in size. 'Knock-back' the dough by re-kneading and punching out any air bubbles, until dough feels smooth. Divide dough into ten pieces. Form each piece into a ball with the fingers and place well apart on greased baking sheets. (Keep unworked pieces of dough covered while shaping buns, to prevent drying out.) Cover with greased polythene or plastic cling wrap, and leave to rise in a warm place until doubled in size. Preheat oven to 220°C (425°F)/Gas 7. Bake buns on second from top shelf of oven for about 15 minutes, until golden brown. To test if cooked, tap buns underneath; they should sound hollow. Place on a wire rack to cool. Mix sugar and milk together, brush glaze over buns whilst still hot.

Apricot Crescent

This is an unusual cake dessert, faintly reminiscent of a Danish pastry. Serve it with hot custard or cream as a dessert, or cold, in slices as a not too sweet cake for afternoon tea.

400g (1 lb) plain flour
2.5ml (½ teaspoon) salt
25g (1 oz) fresh yeast
25g (1 oz) caster sugar
30ml (2 tablespoons) hand-hot milk
75g (3 oz) butter

2 (size 2) eggs
75g (3 oz) finely grated stale Cheddar cheese
one 411g (14½ oz) can drained apricots

Warm the bowl, then sieve into it the flour and salt. Cream yeast and sugar together with the back of a spoon, then pour the milk over it. Leave for a few minutes. Rub the butter into the flour. Whisk eggs, add to milk then pour it all into the flour. Mix together until it leaves the sides of the bowl. Turn out on to a floured board and knead it until it becomes smooth and elastic. It is sticky at this stage, but don't use too much extra flour or you will spoil the proportions. Drain the apricots and chop into small pieces. Roll out the dough to a rectangle about 1.5cm (½ in) thick. Sprinkle the apricots evenly over the surface together with remaining cheese. Roll up carefully to make a largish roll. Grease a baking sheet really well and put the roll made into a crescent shape, on it, placing the edges underneath. Cover with greased polythene and leave in a warm place for 20 to 25 minutes until well risen. Preheat oven to 200°C (400°F)/Gas 6 and bake for 25 to 30 minutes. Serve as described above.

Figgy Malt Loaf
I make this with more figs than any other dried fruit, but you can use all raisins or sultanas if you prefer.

25g (1 oz) butter
30ml (2 tablespoons) black treacle
45ml (3 tablespoons) malt extract
25g (1 oz) fresh yeast (or use 15g (½ oz) dried yeast with 5ml
   (1 teaspoon) sugar) with 125ml (5 fl oz) plus 45ml (3 table-
   spoons) warm water
450g (1 lb) plain flour
5ml (1 teaspoon) salt
200g (8 oz) mixture of figs and dried apricots, or use raisins
   sultanas, etc

Melt butter, treacle and malt extract together and stir until blended. Leave on one side to cool. Dissolve yeast in warm water. Cut up figs and dried apricots into small pieces. Sieve flour and salt and add the fruit. Make a well in the centre and add the treacle mixture and the yeast. Mix to make a soft dough. It is very sticky at this stage and you can add some extra flour if you wish but not too much. Turn on to a floured board and knead until dough is smooth and elastic. Form it into a roll in your hands, then divide roll in two and put each one into a well greased 900g (2 lb) loaf tin. Cover with an oiled polythene bag and leave in a warm place to rise. The loaf will increase to about double its size. Remove bags and bake in the middle of a fairly hot oven, 200°C (400°F)/Gas 6 for about 40 minutes. Glaze while still hot by using a wet brush dipped in honey.

Oatmeal Bread

This dough is rather sticky to knead, and you may need more flour than usual on the board to keep going. The result is a very moist and tasty bread, so persevere.

300g (12 oz) rolled oats
250ml (½ pt) milk
300g (12 oz) wholemeal flour
10ml (2 teaspoons) salt
15g (½ oz) fresh yeast (or 10ml (2 teaspoons) dried yeast and 5ml
(1 teaspoon) sugar)
125ml (¼ pt) warm water
50g (2 oz) melted lard

Put the oats into a large bowl and pour on the milk. Leave for about half an hour until milk is thoroughly absorbed. Add flour and salt. Blend fresh yeast with the warm hand-hot water or if using dried yeast mix yeast with teaspoon of sugar and sprinkle over the warm water. Leave about ten minutes to activate — it will become frothy. Pour the yeast and water on to the flour mixture, together with the melted lard. Beat to bring all the ingredients together — the sides of the bowl will eventually become clean. Transfer to a floured board and knead for about ten minutes. During this time the dough will become smooth and elastic to the touch. Put into a greased polythene bag, seal the edges and leave in a warm place until double in bulk. This can take anything from half an hour to two hours, or even longer if you want to finish it off at a later stage. You can delay the rising up to twelve hours if you put it in a cold larder or refrigerator. Remove the bag and 'knock-back' by kneading the dough for a further few minutes. Shape into two small loaves, or make into individual rolls if you prefer. Put them on to a greased baking sheet and return to the greased polythene bag and leave in a warm place for a further 40 minutes to one hour. Preheat oven to 220°C (425°F)/Gas 7 and bake in the middle of the oven for 25 to 35 minutes depending on the size of the loaves.

Rosemary Bread

Herb breads give an added zing to the bread and cheese lunch especially bread made with wholemeal flour.

> *675g (1½ lb) wholemeal flour*
> *10ml (2 teaspoons) salt*
> *10ml (2 teaspoons) dried rosemary*
> *250ml (½ pt) boiling water*
> *250ml (½ pt) cold water*
> *5ml (1 teaspoon) sugar*
> *1, 25mg vitamin C tablet*
> *25g (1 oz) fresh yeast*
> *25g (1 oz) lard*
> *little milk*

Warm a large mixing bowl. Sieve flour and salt into bowl and stir in the dried rosemary. Mix the boiling and cold water to give the right temperature. Into a bowl put the sugar and vitamin C tablet. Add half the warm water and sprinkle in the yeast. Stir to blend then leave in a warm place for about 20 minutes until a froth appears on top. In the meantime rub the lard into the flour. Add the remaining water to the yeast mixture and pour into the flour. Stir until the mixture leaves the sides of the bowl. Turn out onto a floured board and knead for ten minutes until the dough is smooth and has an elastic touch. Leave to rest for five minutes. Grease a 450g (1 lb) and 900g (2 lb) loaf tin, or make individual rolls if you prefer, in which case grease a baking sheet. Form into rolls or loaves. Wrap in greased polythene and leave in a warm place for about 30 minutes or until well risen. Preheat oven to 230°C (450°F)/Gas 8. Brush tops of loaves with milk. Bake in centre of oven, about 25 minutes for large rolls, or between 30-40 minutes for loaves. The base of the bread should sound hollow when tapped and the loaves will have shrunk slightly from the sides of the tin. Turn out and leave to cool.

Sultana Bread

> *675g (1½ lb) wholemeal flour*
> *7.5ml (1½ teaspoons) salt*
> *25g (1 oz) fresh yeast*
> *25g (1 oz) dark brown sugar*
> *450ml (¾ pt) hand-hot water*
> *30ml (2 rounded tablespoons) black treacle*
> *100g (4 oz) sultanas*

136

Sift flour and salt into a warm bowl. Mix yeast with sugar and pour over it the hot water. Stir to dissolve. Pour into the flour with the treacle and sultanas and mix until the dough leaves the sides of the bowl. Transfer to a floured board and knead for about ten minutes until dough is smooth and elastic to the touch. Divide mixture into a 900g (2 lb) and 450g (1 lb) greased loaf tin, or make individual rolls and put them on a greased baking tray. Cover with polythene and allow to rise in a warm place until well risen — about 35 minutes. Preheat oven to 200°C (400°F)/Gas 6. Bake in centre of oven for about 45-50 minutes for a loaf or 35-40 minutes for rolls. When cooked bread will have shrunk slightly from the sides of the tin and sound slightly hollow when tapped on the underside. Cool on a wire rack.

Savarin

A savarin is a rich yeast mixture cooked in a ring tin then soaked in syrup after cooking. It can be served with a fruit salad in the centre. The syrup is very often flavoured with kirsch or rum. The soaking in syrup is an important part of the operation, otherwise the mixture may seem heavy. A strong flour is needed because once the water is added the gluten in the flour becomes elastic and will blow up to give a light texture and good volume.

For the batter:

15g (½ oz) fresh yeast or 10ml (2 teaspoons) dried yeast with
    2.5ml (½ teaspoon) sugar
75ml (5 tablespoons) warm milk
25g (1 oz) strong flour

For the remainder:

125g (5 oz) strong flour
1ml (¼ teaspoon) salt
15g (½ oz) caster sugar
3 grade 4 (medium) eggs
75g (3 oz) butter

This is sufficient for two, 15cm (6 in) ring moulds or one 20cm (8 in).

For the sugar syrup:

100g (4 oz) granulated sugar
125ml (¼ pt) water
30ml (2 tablespoons) rum or kirsch to flavour

For the glaze:

30ml (2 tablespoons) apricot jam

Mix the ingredients for the batter and allow to stand until frothy — about 15-20 minutes. Make sure the milk is warm enough — hand hot 43°C (110°F). Sift the remaining flour and salt into a bowl, rub in the butter. Beat the eggs, then add all the ingredients to the yeast liquid. Blend together with a wooden spoon gradually, ensuring it is smooth and not lumpy. Then beat vigorously for three to four minutes. Grease and flour two, 15cm (6 in) ring moulds, or one measuring 20cm (8 in). Pour batter into ring mould (it should be no more than half full) cover with an oiled polythene bag and leave in a warm place until batter has doubled in size. Preheat oven to 200°C (400°F)/Gas 6 and bake savarin near top of oven for 10-15 minutes. Cool for a few minutes, then turn out carefully onto a wire rack. While the sponge is still warm, pour over the syrup. Have a plate underneath so that any excess syrup can be put back into the sponge.

To make the syrup, put granulated sugar into a strong based small saucepan with the water. Heat very slowly until sugar has dissolved, then boil rapidly for two or three minutes. Add kirsch or rum, then spoon carefully over the sponge ring. Finally before serving with either fruit salad piled in the centre or whipped cream flavoured with vanilla, glaze with an apricot glaze. Heat two tablespoons apricot jam until runny, then brush over the sponge.

Yeast Steamed Pudding
This has a different texture from other sponge puddings and is to my mind more filling. You can add sultanas (about 150g (6 oz)) if you wish.

200g (8 oz) plain flour
50g (2 oz) semolina
50g (2 oz) caster sugar
2.5ml (½ teaspoon) salt
75g (3 oz) butter
25g (1 oz) fresh yeast or 15ml (1 tablespoon) dried yeast and 2.5ml
   (½ teaspoon) sugar
2 (grade 2) eggs
75ml (5 tablespoons) milk

Sieve flour, add semolina, sugar, salt and rub in butter until mixture resembles fine breadcrumbs. Rub fresh yeast into the mix.

Add eggs and milk and mix thoroughly until blended. (If using dried yeast heat milk to warm, then dissolve the sugar in it and sprinkle the yeast on top. Leave to activate — it will become frothy after about ten minutes, then add to mixture with the eggs.) Pour into a well greased 1 litre (2 pt) basin. Leave covered with a damp cloth in a warm place for about an hour, until the mixture has risen. Cover with greaseproof paper or foil with a pleat over the centre to allow the pudding to rise. Put in a saucepan of cold water and bring to the boil slowly. Steam for 1½ hours. Turn out of the basin onto a warmed plate and serve with custard or golden syrup or a jam sauce.

Kugelhopf

15g (½ oz) blanched, sliced almonds
25g (¾ oz) scant fresh yeast or 45ml (3 level teaspoons) dried yeast
200ml (8 fl oz) warm milk
100g (4 oz) butter
300g (12 oz) strong plain white flour
2.5ml (½ level teaspoon) salt
25g (1 oz) caster sugar
100g (4 oz) mixed dried fruit
2 eggs
icing sugar to dredge

Grease a 17.5cm to 20cm (7 to 8 in) diameter kugelhopf tin well, and press the almonds around sides and bottom of tin. Crumble fresh yeast into warm milk and stir to dissolve. (If using dried yeast, dissolve 5ml (1 level teaspoon) caster sugar in 200ml (8 fl oz) hand-hot milk. Sprinkle dried yeast on top and leave about ten minutes until frothy.) Melt butter and allow to cool slightly. Mix flour, salt, sugar and dried fruit in a bowl. Beat eggs and add to flour with yeast liquid and butter. Beat mixture well with a wooden spoon, and pour into tin so it is three-quarters full. Cover with greased polythene, foil or plastic cling wrap, and leave to rise in a warm place until mixture is about 2.5cm (1 in) below top of tin. Preheat oven to 190°C (375°F)/Gas 5 and bake in centre of oven for about 50 minutes. If the top browns too much, cover with foil until cooked. Test with a skewer before removing from oven; there should be no dough sticking to skewer if it is cooked. Leave in tin a few minutes, then turn out and cool on a wire rack. Dredge top with icing sugar.
    Good served in slices with coffee.

Spiced Cloverleaves
Makes 12

15g (½ oz) fresh yeast or 10ml (2 level teaspoons) dried yeast
150ml (6 fl oz) warm milk
300g (¾ lb) strong plain white flour
5ml (1 level teaspoon) salt
15g (½ oz) margarine
50g (2 oz) mixed dried fruit
15g (½ oz) caster sugar
2.5ml (½ level teaspoon) cinnamon
1ml (¼ level teaspoon) nutmeg
1 egg

For the topping:

15g (½ oz) butter
15g (½ oz) soft brown sugar
15ml (1 level tablespoon) golden syrup
few chopped nuts and raisins

Crumble fresh yeast into warm milk and stir to dissolve. (If using dried yeast, dissolve 5ml (1 level teaspoon) caster sugar in 150ml (6 fl oz) hand-hot milk. Sprinkle dried yeast on top and leave about ten minutes until frothy.) Mix flour and salt in a bowl and rub in margarine. Stir in mixed dried fruit, caster sugar and spices. Beat egg and mix with yeast liquid into flour. Turn out dough and sprinkle surface lightly with flour if dough is at all sticky. Knead dough, stretching and folding, until it feels firm and elastic and no longer sticky. Place dough in a lightly greased bowl, cover with greased polythene, foil or plastic cling wrap, and leave to rise in a warm place until doubled in size.

To make the topping, melt butter and stir in sugar and syrup. Scatter a few chopped nuts and raisins in the base of a twelve-holed tartlet tin. Place a little of the butter syrup in each one. 'Knock-back' the dough by re-kneading and punching out any air bubbles, until dough feels smooth. Divide dough into twelve pieces. Cut each piece into three. (Keep unworked pieces of dough covered while shaping buns, to prevent drying out.) Form each piece into a small ball with the fingers. For each cloverleaf, place three of the small balls into each tartlet case. Cover with greased polythene or plastic cling wrap, and leave to rise in a warm place until doubled in size. Preheat oven to 200°C (400°F)/Gas 6. Bake buns in centre of oven for 15-20

140

minutes, until golden brown. Turn out straight away or buns will stick, and place on a wire rack to cool, sticky side up.

Treacle and Ginger Loaf

> *200g (8 oz) wholewheat flour*
> *200g (8 oz) strong white flour*
> *10ml (2 teaspoons) sugar*
> *10ml (2 teaspoons) salt*
> *15g (½ oz) fresh yeast or 10ml (2 teaspoons) dried yeast*
> *250ml (½ pt) warm water*
> *15g (½ oz) lard*
> *30ml (2 tablespoons) black treacle*
> *25g (1 oz) margarine*
> *10ml (2 teaspoons) ground ginger*
> *50g (2 oz) currants*

To glaze:

> *30ml (2 tablespoons) orange jelly marmalade*

If using fresh yeast, sift flour, salt and sugar together. Rub in the lard. Blend yeast in the water and pour into the flour. Mix to a dough that leaves the bowl clean. If using dried yeast, dissolve 5ml (1 teaspoon) of the sugar in a cupful of warm water used in recipe. Sprinkle dried yeast on top. Leave until frothy, about 10 minutes. Sift flour salt and remaining sugar together and rub in lard. Add yeast liquid with rest of water to flour and mix to a dough. Knead dough thoroughly until smooth. Place dough in a lightly oiled polythene bag, loosely tied, and allow to rise in a warm place until doubled in size. Replace dough in mixing bowl and add remaining ingredients. Squeeze all the ingredients together until the mixture is no longer streaky. Shape dough and place in a greased small 450g (1 lb) loaf tin. Put tin inside a greased polythene bag to rise until it is within 1cm (½ in) from the top of the tin (about 1 hour in a warm place). Bake at 200°C (400°F)/Gas 6 for 40 minutes. Cool. To glaze, heat marmalade gently in a small size pan and use it to brush top of loaf. Serve sliced with butter.

Ginger Marmalade Squares

> *25g (1 oz) fresh yeast or 15ml (1 level tablespoon) dried yeast*

150ml (6 fl oz) warm milk
400g (1 lb) strong plain white flour
2.5ml (½ level teaspoon) salt
75g (3 oz) soft brown sugar
75g (3 oz) butter
1 egg

For the topping:

25g (1 oz) butter
50g (2 oz) soft brown sugar
15g (½ oz) plain flour
15ml (3 level teaspoons) ground ginger
30ml (2 level tablespoons) ginger marmalade

Crumble fresh yeast into warm milk and stir to dissolve. (If using dried yeast, dissolve 5ml (1 level teaspoon) caster sugar in 150ml (6 fl oz) hand-hot milk. Sprinkle dried yeast on top and leave about ten minutes until frothy.) Mix flour, salt and sugar in a bowl. Melt butter and allow to cool slightly. Beat the egg and mix with melted butter and yeast liquid into flour. Turn out dough and sprinkle surface lightly with flour if dough is at all sticky. Knead dough, stretching and folding until it feels firm and elastic and no longer sticky. Place dough in a lightly greased bowl, cover with greased polythene, foil or plastic cling wrap, and leave to rise in a warm place until doubled in size.

For the topping, melt butter and stir in sugar, flour and ginger. 'Knock-back' the dough by re-kneading and punching out any air bubbles, until dough feels smooth. Divide dough in half and roll each piece out to a 20cm (8 in) square. Press one half into base of a 20cm (8 in) square, deep cake tin and sprinkle half the topping over. Press other half of dough on top, cover with greased polythene or plastic cling wrap, and leave to rise in a warm place until doubled in size. Preheat oven to 200°C (400°F)/Gas 6. Spread the ginger marmalade carefully over top of dough, sprinkle over remaining topping, and bake in centre of oven for 45-50 minutes. If the top begins to brown too much, cover with foil until cooked. Test with a skewer before removing from oven; there should be no dough sticking to skewer if cooked. Place on a wire rack to cool. Serve cut into squares or slices.

Croissants
Makes 12 to 14

25g (1 oz) fresh yeast or 15ml (1 level tablespoon) dried yeast
175ml plus 15ml (½ pint less 4 tablespoons) warm water
400g (1 lb) strong plain white flour
10ml (2 level teaspoons) salt
25g (1 oz) margarine
1 egg
125g (5 oz) hard margarine

For the glaze:

1 egg
2.5ml (½ level teaspoon) caster sugar
5ml (1 teaspoon) water

Crumble fresh yeast into warm water and stir to dissolve. (If using dried yeast, dissolve 5ml (1 level teaspoon) caster sugar in hand-hot water. Sprinkle dried yeast on top and leave about ten minutes until frothy.) Mix flour and salt and rub in 25g (1 oz) margarine. Beat egg and mix with yeast liquid into flour. Turn out dough and sprinkle surface lightly with flour if dough is at all sticky. Knead dough, stretching and folding, until it feels firm and elastic and no longer sticky. Roll the dough to an oblong about 50cm x 20cm (20 x 8 in) keeping the edges as straight as possible. Divide the 125g (5 oz) margarine into three, and dot one-third over two-thirds of the dough, leaving the edges clear. Fold the dough in three, bringing the uncovered piece of dough over first. Seal edges with a rolling pin. Turn dough so fold is to the right. Carefully re-roll dough again as before, repeating with other two portions of margarine and folding twice more. Place dough in a greased polythene bag or plastic cling wrap and allow to rest in refrigerator for 30 minutes. Roll out as before and repeat rolling and folding three more times, this time without adding the fat. Wrap and leave in refrigerator at least one hour. Beat together the egg, sugar and water.

For shaping, roll dough to an oblong about 57.5cm by 35cm (23 x 14 in) and cut in half lengthwise. Divide each strip into six triangles about 15cm (6 in) high with a 15cm (6 in) base. Brush glaze over the pieces of dough. Roll up each triangle from the base to tip, loosely. Place croissants on ungreased baking sheets. Cover with greased polythene or plastic cling wrap, and leave to rise in a warm place until doubled in size and puffy (about 30 minutes). Preheat oven to

143

220°C (425°F)/Gas 7. Brush croissants with glaze and bake in centre of oven about 20 minutes until golden brown.

Croissants are best served warm.

Potato Bread Plait

4 rashers streaky bacon
15g (½ oz) fresh yeast or 10ml (2 level teaspoons) dried yeast
150ml (6 fl oz) warm water
250g (10 oz) strong plain white flour
100g (4 oz) wholemeal flour
5ml (1 level teaspoon) salt
2.5ml (½ level teaspoon) caster sugar
15g (½ oz) margarine
150g (6 oz) cold mashed potato
5ml (1 level teaspoon) mixed dried herbs
beaten egg or milk to glaze
poppy seeds

Grill bacon rashers and crumble into small pieces. Leave to cool. Crumble fresh yeast into warm water and stir to dissolve. (If using dried yeast, dissolve 5ml (1 level teaspoon) caster sugar in 150ml (6 fl oz) hand-hot water. Sprinkle dried yeast on top and leave about ten minutes until frothy.) Mix flours, salt and sugar in a bowl and rub in margarine. Mix mashed potato into flour with herbs and bacon. Mix yeast extract into flour, adding a little extra flour if needed. Turn out dough and sprinkle surface lightly with flour if dough is at all sticky. Knead dough, stretching and folding until it feels firm and elastic and no longer sticky. Place dough in a lightly greased bowl, cover with greased polythene, foil or plastic cling wrap, and leave to rise in a warm place until doubled in size. 'Knock-back' the dough by re-kneading and punching out any air bubbles, until dough feels smooth. Divide dough into three and roll each piece with the hands to a 35cm (14 in) long strip. Gather together one end of each roll and press firmly together. Plait half-way down, then turn over and complete plaiting. Seal ends and tuck underneath. Place on a greased baking sheet. Cover with greased polythene or plastic cling wrap, and leave to rise in a warm place until doubled in size. Preheat oven to 220°C (425°F)/Gas 7. Brush top of plait with beaten egg or milk, and sprinkle with poppy seeds. Bake in centre of oven for about 25 minutes until golden brown. To test if cooked, tap loaf underneath; it should sound hollow. Place on a wire rack to cool.

N.B. For a plain potato loaf, omit the bacon and herbs. The addition of potato makes this a soft textured bread. It is good served warm with cheese or meats.

Apricot and Walnut Teabread

75g (3 oz) dried apricots
50g (2 oz) dates
50g (2 oz) walnuts (reserve 3 or 4 to decorate)
15g (½ oz) fresh yeast or 10ml (2 level teaspoons) dried yeast
125ml (¼ pt) less 15ml (1 tablespoon) warm water
100g (4 oz) strong plain white flour
75g (3 oz) wheatmeal flour
25g (1 oz) wheatgerm
2.5ml (½ level teaspoon) salt
15g (½ oz) margarine
15ml (1 level tablespoon) clear honey
100g (4 oz) icing sugar

Chop dried apricots, dates and walnuts. Crumble fresh yeast into warm water and stir to dissolve. (If using dried yeast, dissolve 5ml (1 level teaspoon) caster sugar in the hand-hot water. Sprinkle dried yeast on top and leave about ten minutes until frothy.) Mix flours, wheatgerm, and salt in a bowl and rub in margarine. Stir in apricots, dates and walnuts. Mix yeast liquid into flour with honey. Turn out dough and sprinkle surface lightly with flour if dough is at all sticky. Knead dough, stretching and folding, until it feels firm and elastic and no longer sticky. Place dough in a lightly greased bowl, cover with greased polythene, foil or plastic cling wrap, and leave to rise in a warm place until doubled in size. 'Knock-back' the dough by re-kneading and punching out any air bubbles, until dough feels smooth. Flatten the dough to the width and length of a greased 450g (1 lb) loaf tin, and press in. Cover with greased polythene or plastic cling wrap, and leave to rise in a warm place until doubled in size, or dough reaches just above the top of the tin. Preheat oven to 200°C (400°F)/Gas 6. Bake loaf in centre of oven for 25 to 30 minutes; cover with foil if loaf browns too quickly. To test if cooked, tap loaf underneath; it should sound hollow. Place on a wire rack to cool. Mix icing sugar with 30ml (2 tablespoons) water and pour over top of teabread. Roughly chop extra walnuts to decorate.

Hot Cross Buns

675g (1½ lb) strong plain flour
5ml (1 level teaspoon) salt
25g (1 oz) fresh yeast or 15ml (1 level tablespoon) dried yeast
100g (4 oz) caster sugar
375ml (¾ pt) milk
100g (4 oz) margarine
5ml (1 teaspoon) mixed spice
2 (grade 2) eggs
100g (4 oz) currants
50g (2 oz) mixed peel

For the glaze:

50g (2 oz) caster sugar

Sieve 100g (4 oz) of the flour with salt into a warm bowl. Cream yeast with 5ml (1 teaspoon) of the sugar. Heat milk until tepid to warm. Pour milk over yeast and sugar then add to flour slowly, beating well. Cover with a damp cloth and put in a warm place for half an hour to ferment. Bubbles will appear on the surface and it will take on a frothy appearance. Rub fat into remaining flour and add sugar and mixed spice. Beat eggs until yolk and white are blended. Pour fermented mixture slowly in to flour beating well, add eggs, stir in currants and peel. Beat well until mixture is smooth and leaves the sides of the bowl cleanly. Turn onto a floured board, knead until mixture is soft and smooth but not sticky. Cover with a damp cloth, set in a warm place until doubled in size — about half an hour. Knock back and shape into 20 buns and put them on greased baking trays leaving plenty of space between. Set them to rise again in a warm place until doubled in size — about 30 minutes. Just before baking mark a cross on the top of each bun. Bake at 200°C (400°F)/Gas 6 for about 15 minutes. Leave to cool on a wire rack and while still hot glaze with 50g (2 oz) sugar melted in 45ml (3 tablespoons) hot water and brought to the boil. Brush over tops of buns and allow to cool.

Danish Pastries
Makes 16

15g (½ oz) fresh yeast or 10ml (2 level teaspoons) dried yeast
90ml (6 tablespoons) warm water
200g (8 oz) strong plain flour

1ml (¼ level teaspoon) salt
15g (½ oz) margarine
15ml (1 level tablespoon) caster sugar
1 egg
125g (5 oz) butter

For the custard filling:

15ml (1 level tablespoon) plain flour
5ml (1 level teaspoon) cornflour
1 egg yolk
15ml (1 level tablespoon) caster sugar
125ml (¼ pt) milk
few drops vanilla essence

For the almond paste:

50g (2 oz) ground almonds
50g (2 oz) caster sugar
3 drops almond essence
little egg white

beaten egg or milk to glaze
glacé icing
flaked almonds
glacé cherries

Crumble fresh yeast into warm water and stir to dissolve. (If using dried yeast, dissolve 5ml (1 level teaspoon) caster sugar in hand-hot water. Sprinkle dried yeast on top and leave about ten minutes until frothy.) Mix flour and salt in a bowl and rub in the 15g (½ oz) margarine. Stir in sugar. Beat egg and mix with yeast liquid into flour. Turn out dough and sprinkle surface lightly with flour if dough is at all sticky. Knead dough lightly until smooth. Place dough in a polythene bag or plastic cling wrap and leave to rest in refrigerator for ten minutes. Beat the butter until soft. Roll the dough to about a 25cm (10 in) square. Spread butter in centre of the dough, leaving 1.25cm (½ in) clear at each side, and about 5cm (2 in) clear at each end. Fold the unbuttered ends over so they just overlap; seal all the edges. Turn the dough and roll to an oblong about 37.5cm by 12.5cm (15 x 5 in). Fold the dough evenly in three. Wrap and leave in refrigerator for ten minutes (or until the butter is firm). Repeat rolling and folding twice more, then wrap and rest dough for about ten minutes. Prepare fillings. For the custard filling, mix the flours, egg yolk and sugar together with a little of the milk. Bring the rest of the milk just to boil and stir well into the mixture. Return to the heat and stir until just boiling. Remove from heat and add a few drops of vanilla essence. Cool; cover with greaseproof paper to prevent a skin forming. For the almond paste, mix ground almonds and sugar together. Stir in almond essence and sufficient lightly beaten egg white to make a smooth paste. Divide the dough in half and for making the pastries in the shape of stars and envelopes follow this procedure:

Roll half the dough to a rectangle about 15cm by 30cm (6 x 12 in) and divide into eight squares. For Stars: place a little almond paste in the centre of four squares. Cut each corner to within 1.25cm (½ in) of the centre and fold alternate corners onto the almond paste, overlapping each other. Place on a baking sheet and brush with beaten egg or milk. For Envelopes: place a little almond paste or custard in centre of four squares. Fold all the corners to the centre and press down well. Place on a baking sheet and brush with beaten egg or milk. For making crescent shapes roll remaining half of dough to a 23cm (9 in) circle and cut into eight sections. Place a little almond paste or custard in the middle, roll up towards the point, and curl into a crescent shape. Place on a baking sheet and brush with beaten egg or milk. Preheat oven to 220°C (425°F)/Gas 7. Leave pastries in a slightly warm place until puffy, about 20 minutes. (Do not leave in too warm a place or the fat will run out and spoil the pastry.) Bake the pastries on second from top shelf of oven for 10-15 minutes. Fill the corners of envelopes with custard and return to oven for one minute. Ice pastries with glacé icing whilst still warm, and sprinkle stars and crescents with flaked almonds, and decorate envelopes with pieces of glacé cherry.

Nutty Wheatgerm Rolls
Makes 10 to 12

15g (½ oz) fresh yeast or 10ml (2 level teaspoons) dried yeast
scant 200ml (8 fl oz) warm water
225g (9 oz) wheatmeal flour
75g (3 oz) wheatgerm
25g (1 oz) bran
5ml (1 level teaspoon) salt
15g (½ oz) margarine
15ml (1 level tablespoon) black treacle

Crumble fresh yeast into warm water and stir to dissolve. (If using dried yeast dissolve 5ml (1 level teaspoon) caster sugar in scant 200ml (8 fl oz) hand-hot water. Sprinkle dried yeast on top and leave about ten minutes until frothy.) Mix flour, wheatgerm, bran and salt in a bowl and rub in margarine. Mix yeast liquid into flour with treacle. Turn out dough and sprinkle surface lightly with flour if dough is at all sticky, adding more flour if necessary. Place dough in a lightly greased bowl, cover with greased polythene, foil or plastic cling wrap, and leave to rise in a warm place until doubled in size. 'Knock-back' the dough by re-kneading and punching out any air bubbles until dough feels smooth. Divide dough into ten or twelve pieces. Form each piece into a ball with the fingers and place well apart on greased baking sheets. (Keep unworked pieces of dough covered while shaping rolls, to prevent drying out.) Cover with greased polythene or plastic cling wrap, and leave to rise in a warm place until doubled in size. Preheat oven to 230°C (450°F)/Gas 8. Sprinkle rolls with a little wheatmeal flour and bake on second from top shelf of oven for 10-15 minutes until golden brown. To test if cooked, tap rolls underneath; they should sound hollow. Place on a wire rack to cool.

Cheesy Tomato Roll Loaf

15g (½ oz) fresh yeast or 10ml (2 teaspoons) dried yeast and
    5ml (1 teaspoon) sugar
250ml (½ pt) warm water
125g (5 oz) tomato purée
600g (1½ lb) strong white flour
15g (½ oz) salt
15g (½ oz) lard
100g (4 oz) grated Cheddar cheese

If using fresh yeast, blend yeast with half the warm water. If using dried yeast, dissolve sugar in half the water, sprinkle dried yeast on top and leave until frothy, about 10 minutes. Blend the tomato purée with the remaining water. Sift flour and salt together and rub in lard. Pour yeast and tomato liquids into dry ingredients and knead for about 10 minutes to form a smooth dough. Place in an oiled polythene bag, loosely tied, and allow to rise in a warm place until doubled in size. Turn dough on to a lightly floured surface, flatten and incorporate half the cheese by kneading. Divide into twelve equal-sized pieces. Shape each piece into a smooth ball. Grease two 15cm (6 in) sandwich tins and arrange 5 dough balls in each tin to form a ring. Place the two remaining balls in the centre of each tin. Brush with milk. Cover with oiled polythene and leave to rise until doubled in size, about 30 minutes in a warm place. Remove polythene. Bake at 220°C (425°F)/Gas 7 for 30-35 minutes in all. Sprinkle remaining cheese on top of each loaf after 20 minutes of the baking time.

Pizza dough

Basic recipe to make two pizzas, each serving four to six people.

> *450g (1 lb) plain flour*
> *10ml (2 teaspoons) salt*
> *15g (½ oz) lard*
> *15g (½ oz) fresh yeast (for dried yeast see note below)*
> *250ml (½ pt) hand-hot water*

Sieve flour and salt into a bowl. Rub in lard until mixture resembles fine breadcrumbs. Dissolve yeast in the warm water, stir well. Mix liquid with the flour and work until dough is smooth and leaves the sides of the bowl clean. Turn out on to a floured board and knead until dough is firm and springs back when pulled. This takes about ten minutes (no less, so don't cheat). Lightly oil a polythene bag and put in the dough. Fold over top of bag and leave to double in size. This will take about an hour in a warm place, two hours at room temperature, 24 hours in a refrigerator. If the dough has been refrigerated it must return to room temperature before shaping.

For finishings and toppings, see individual recipes.

NOTE: For dried yeast, dissolve 2.5ml (½ teaspoon) sugar in 250ml (½ pt) hand-hot water and sprinkle over 10ml (2 teaspoons) dried yeast. Leave until frothy — about ten minutes. If it doesn't froth, the yeast is no longer active and you should buy a fresh supply.

Gabriella's Pizza
This was the recipe given to me by an Italian girl and it is one of the most typical pizzas of all.

> *450g (1 lb) basic dough*
> *450g (1 lb) tomatoes*
> *100g (4 oz) Bel Paesa*
> *can anchovy fillets*

151

12 black olives
seasoning
5ml (1 tablespoon) olive oil

Divide dough into two rounds. Skin tomatoes by dipping them in boiling water for a few seconds. The skin can then be peeled off easily. Slice the cheese thinly. Drain anchovy fillets. On to each round put a layer of thickly sliced tomatoes, then cheese, followed by a lattice of anchovy fillets with an olive pressed into each hole. Season well and brush with oil. Bake at 230°C (450°F)/Gas 8 for 20 minutes. Serve with green salad tossed in a sharp French dressing.

Spinach and Frankfurter Pizza

450g (1 lb) basic dough
6 frankfurters
1 medium size onion
450g (1 lb) spinach
seasoning

Divide the basic dough into two rounds. Slice frankfurters in two lengthwise. Chop onion finely. Wash spinach carefully and shake off excess water. Put into a saucepan with a closely fitting lid and cook over a low heat. Shake from time to time to avoid it sticking to the pan. Press between two plates to expel excess moisture. On to each dough round put half the spinach, sprinkle over the chopped onion then place six frankfurter halves in a wheel shape over. Season well. Bake at 230°C (450°F)/Gas 8 for about 20 minutes.

Fisherman's Pizza

½ basic pizza dough mixture
1 can tuna fish
50g (2 oz) mushrooms
1 can anchovy fillets
12 black olives

Make up the dough as described. Drain oil from tuna fish, flake with a fork and spread over the top. Add chopped mushrooms and arrange anchovy fillets over and the olives in rows. Pour over a few drops of olive or vegetable oil to moisten and bake for about 20 minutes at 220°C (425°F)/Gas 7.

Italian Pizzas

basic dough
100g (4 oz) ham
100g (4 oz) salami
1 oz grated Parmesan cheese
seasoning
beaten egg for brushing dough

Make the pizza dough as described in the basic dough recipe. Divide the risen dough into six pieces and knead each one well. Allow to rest for about ten minutes, covered with a damp cloth. Roll each piece into a 15cm (6 in) diameter. Cut the ham and salami into small cm size pieces and, dividing the mixture equally, put it in the centre of the dough. Add the grated cheese. Season well. Dampen the edges of each round and seal together, forming into a semi circle. Snip across the top with scissors and brush with beaten egg. Place on a baking sheet, cover with oiled polythene and leave in a warm place to rest for about ten minutes. Preheat oven to 220°C (425°F)/Gas 7 and bake for 20-25 minutes.

For the tomato sauce:

1 x 397g (14 oz) can tomatoes
1 onion
5ml (1 teaspoon) dried oregano
seasoning

Put all ingredients into a saucepan and simmer until liquid has reduced to a thick sauce. Pour into a sauce dish and serve with the pizzas.

Index

155

157